UEA

Creative Writing
Anthology **2009**

Prose,
Life Writing,
Scriptwriting

egg b•x

UEA Creative Writing Anthology 2009
Prose, Life Writing, Scriptwriting

First published by Egg Box Publishing, 2009.

International © retained by individual authors.

This book is sold subject to the condition that it shall not, by way of trade or otherwise, be lent, resold, hired out, stored in a retrieval system, or otherwise circulated without the publisher's prior consent in any form of binding or cover other than that in which it is published and without a similar condition including this condition being imposed on the subsequent purchaser.

A CIP record for this book is available from the British Library.

UEA Creative Writing Anthology 2009 is typeset in Oranda 10.5pt on 13pt Leading.

Printed and bound by:
the MPG Books Group, Bodmin and King' Lynn

Designed and typeset by:
Kettle of Fish Design, Norwich
www.kettleoffishdesign.com

Proofed by:
Sarah Gooderson

Distributed by:
Central Books

ISBN:
978-0955939938

Acknowledgements

UEA Creative Writing Anthology 2009

Thanks to the following for making this anthology possible: the Malcolm Bradbury Memorial Fund, the Centre for Creative and Performing Arts at the University of East Anglia and The School of Literature & Creative Writing at UEA in partnership with Egg Box Publishing.

We'd also like to thank the following people:

Trezza Azzopardi, Amit Chaudhuri, Jon Cook, Andrew Cowan, Mark Currie, Siân Evans, Giles Foden, Lavinia Greenlaw, Sarah Gooderson, Rachel Hore, Kathryn Hughes, Michael Lengsfield, Jean McNeil, Denise Riley, Rob Ritchie, Michèle Roberts, Val Striker, George Szirtes and Val Taylor.

Nathan Hamilton at Egg Box Publishing, and Catrin & Dylan Lloyd-Edwards at Kettle of Fish Design.

Editorial team:
Chris Astwood
Sue Healy
Alex Lewis
Jake Marcet
James Midgley
Philippa Stewart
Gareth Watkins
Jennifer Wong

UEA Creative Writing Anthology 2009

Contents

Foreword
Tracy Chevalier i

Prose
Introduction – Andrew Cowan 8

Contributors
Ashley Anderson 10
Zoë Bolton 16
Nicholas Brookes 21
Dea Brovig 27
Tyona Campbell 33
Gillian Daly 38
Jonathan Gibbs 43
Claire Griffiths 49
Sue Healy 56
Stephen Hepplestone 63
Philip Langeskov 68
Alex Lewis 74
Seònaid MacKay 77
Sarah Marsh 83
Gavin McCrea 88
Priscilla Morris 93
Jack Reynolds 98
Jacob Rollinson 103
Donna Sharpe 109
Gareth Watkins 114
Kristian White 122
Nisha Woolfstein 129

Life Writing
Introduction – Kathryn Hughes 136

Contributors
Philippa Stewart 138

Scriptwriting
Introduction – Val Taylor 144

Contributors
Drew Castalia 146
Ben Craib 157
Chris Duffill 161
Jake Marcet 177
Ruth Selwyn-Crome 192
William Simpson 205
Andrew Strike 222
Sunitha Webster 235

UEA Creative Writing Anthology 2009

Foreword

by **Tracy Chevalier**

How do you learn to take writing seriously?

I hadn't until I did the MA in Creative Writing course at UEA. I used to fit writing into the crevices of my everyday life. I wrote sporadically, at night and at weekends, sometimes taking up to a year to complete a short story. While I enjoyed writing when I got down to it, there were always the distractions and excuses of theatre and pub, of work and travel and fatigue, to keep me from touching pen to paper, fingers to keyboard.

One day I was on the bus to work, leafing through the newspaper, and read an article about the UEA course. When I got to work, before I'd even taken off my coat or had a coffee, my boss chided me about something I hadn't done. As I tried to think of a reply, the thought popped into my head: The hell with this – I'm going to apply for that course and get out of here. All of a sudden – out of sheer cussedness – I made writing into a meaningful part of my life.

I think to write successfully – meaning people want to read more of what you've written – you need four things: time, discipline, humility and that unknown quality I'll call 'spark.' UEA gave me at least one of those things: time. It cleared my diary of any responsibilities other than feeding myself and writing. Suddenly writing was no longer relegated to the crevices of my day; it became my day. Just that in itself made an enormous difference. I began to write better because I wrote a lot more sentences than before, putting the time in, the way pianists practise and athletes run. This I think is the case for would-be writers everywhere, whether you take a course or simply scribble more often in your garret.

Two of the other qualities – discipline and humility – are not necessarily so easily gained from the MA programme. I'm afraid I witnessed the flagrant dismissal of both from some of my peers during my year in Norwich. One fellow student admitted to me that while he was having a great time socially, he had not written one new piece during the year, but was recycling old writing. At least he had the decency to be embarrassed about his lack of discipline.

As for humility, I vividly remember one class in which I questioned another's passage of writing, saying I wasn't sure what he meant. 'If readers don't understand, that's their problem, not mine,' was his reply. He seemed to have no idea how arrogant and obnoxious such an attitude was, and how damaging to his writing. The reader's experience is the other half of writing; without the reader, writing is masturbation rather than sex. It is no surprise that that student has not gone on to publish.

When I was sitting in class, I sometimes entertained myself by pretending to be a publisher and choosing which of the 18 of us I would sign up. I left myself out of the exercise, but I have to say that the two I chose have indeed both gone on to be published novelists. I don't think this is down to psychic powers on my part. It just seemed clear to me that both had what it took to succeed. They both worked hard, writing a lot and often. (It was no coincidence that both had been out of university several years and had worked as journalists, so were used to deadlines.) They were also open to criticism, willing to accept that what they had written could be improved upon, that their judgment wasn't always right. Finally, both had that elusive spark – the thing that is impossible to teach, and makes your writing sing.

I am generously going to assume that the contributors to this anthology have put in the time, worked hard, and have the humility to accept editing, and that it will show when you read their work. Not all will have the spark, though. However, given past track records for the UEA course, two or three will, and you will hear more from them.

I wish you happy reading, and them happy writing.

TC

UEA Creative Writing Anthology 2009

Prose

Introduction by **Andrew Cowan**

Ashley Anderson
Zoë Bolton
Nicholas Brookes
Dea Brovig
Tyona Campbell
Gillian Daly
Jonathan Gibbs
Claire Griffiths
Sue Healy
Stephen Hepplestone
Philip Langeskov

Alex Lewis
Seònaid MacKay
Sarah Marsh
Gavin McCrea
Priscilla Morris
Jack Reynolds
Jacob Rollinson
Donna Sharpe
Gareth Watkins
Kristian White
Nisha Woolfstein

In his novel *The Wrench* Primo Levi laments the lack of sensitive instrumentation available for the writer to evaluate the 'trueness' of his or her sentences. There's nothing even as rudimentary as a T-square or a plumbline to reveal whether a page is 'right on the bubble'. Consequently writers tend to live on their nerves, in a state of perpetual uncertainty. No wonder, he suggests, that they 'live badly, are melancholy, drink, smoke, can't sleep, and die young.'

For the best of our students this will merely confirm something they already know, that the writer is always alone in the language, with no one to blame if his or her writing goes wrong – 'that page is your work,' says Levi, 'only yours: you have no excuses or pretexts; you are totally responsible.'

There is that. But another reason for invoking Levi is to argue, if only temporarily, against him. One attraction of a course such as ours is that it offers new writers an opportunity to test their pages against the makeshift instrumentation of the workshop. For one privileged year at least they needn't live badly, or be melancholy. They will have the benefit of twelve other pairs of squinting eyes, twelve other perspectives on the trueness of their pages.

This has certainly been the case on this year's MA, whose students have proved to be some of the best critics of each other's writing, generous not only in their encouragement, but in the intensity of their critical engagement with each other's work and in their commitment to helping each other develop.

The quality of the writing collected here – a snapshot of where they were mid-way through the course – suggests the likelihood of their emerging as some of the best writers to have done our course, too.

AC

Ashley Anderson

Lay the Parade
An extract from a novel

The below section is from a novel I am working on currently titled Lay The Parade. It is about a Canadian girl who comes to London to escape her family troubles and to form a band. While in London she meets an array of odd characters, pursues her musical ambitions, and befriends a celebrity musician with whom she has been obsessed for years.

***

The Docklands Light Rail trains lumber like leviathans through the station. Their bellies slide open, people emerge, people disappear, and the trains lumber on. The air is dull here, though Canary Wharf station is open at both ends – it is like a jar that was sealed long ago, bleached by sun and time. Far above, raindrops splinter off the glass roof.

The doors open with a loud digital ding, and she sits on a bench in the nearly vacant front car. She watches the tracks as the train begins to move, now more like a children's rollercoaster. Everything in Canary Wharf is new and shiny compared to the rest of London. It is the part of London most like North America, but it seems the most without character to her. Like Narcissus, it watches its brilliant self in the locks and pools of the docklands.

'Name of a German town ...'

On the front bench, two women sit with bent heads, mulling over a crossword puzzle.

'Which German town?'

'Well that's what we have to figure out, isn't it?'
'Mmm ...'
'Starts with an "s" ... I'm sure it starts with an "s".'
'Are you sure?'
'Yes, I'm sure it starts with an "s".'
'Hmm ... no, nope, that couldn't be it.'
'No, no, that's not it.'
From behind them, a young man leans forward, his arm straining over his girlfriend's shoulders. 'How many letters?'
The women turn and look at him.
'We were just in Germany, so we might know,' he says.
'Seven. Seven letters.'
'Stuttgart?'
'Well, that's nine letters, isn't it?'
He leans back in his seat. 'Saxony?'
'No, well, that's a state, isn't it? S... Sch... Schw...'
'Schwerin?'
'No,' they say in unison. 'No, it should be. Do you know a lot of German towns?'
'No, we were just traveling around.'
'Well, it may not be a German town.'
'No, it may not be a German town.'
'Wait a minute. Where are we?'
They look up, searching over their heads for a sign, fixing on the pixel board. 'Oh, Crossharbour. We've got miles to go.'
'What's the one with the "d" then?'
'I mean, there could be an "i" there, couldn't there?'
'Yes, but the whole thing has to relate to "shrub", to the word "shrub".'
'No, I haven't seen that done with "shrub".'
'No, I haven't.'
'What's a three-letter word for a set of musical notes?'
'Key!' She calls from her seat, and they all turn to look at her, the women on the front bench and the young guy with his girlfriend beneath his wing. She looks back, her face flushing.
'Uh, yes. Thank you,' one of the women says. They turn back around. 'Now, this is why I thought it was a German town ...'

Ashley Anderson

Lewisham is the last stop. She gets off and struggles with her bag on the sidewalk, pulling from it the piece of paper with her scrawled handwriting. She holds the paper in one hand, and the map she printed from the internet in the other.

She follows the map a few streets over and a few streets up, house to house, until she is in front of a brown row house. She stands in front of the tempered glass of the door for a moment before ringing the bell. A tall thin man with lanky blond hair opens the door, reaching down to push back a black cat and holding it behind him with one foot before looking at her. He blinks.

'Hi. I'm Josephine. I called about the room.'

He nods. 'I'm Riddin. Come in.' He pulls the door wide, exposing a deep blue entranceway with tiny stars painted on the ceiling. 'I'll show you the room first.' He leads her up the staircase, past framed photos of unicorns and dragons, and small shelves crammed with figurines of wizards holding crystal balls.

On the landing two spacious bedrooms are visible behind open doors. He turns and opens a narrow door on the side to reveal a large closet with a small window high up the wall. It is filled waist-high with small cellophane packages. She reaches down to pick one up. It is a doll in plastic wrapping.

'We sell those at the conventions. Obviously those will be cleared out. We'll put a single bed in here.'

'Conventions?' She turns the doll in her hand. It is wearing a pointed hat and cape. She looks down. All of the dolls are dressed the same.

'Yes. I'm a warlock.'

'You're a warlock?'

'That's right.'

'Oh.' He watches her place the doll back on the pile, feign an interested glance around the little room. He closes the door and leads her down the stairs.

In the living room a short man with ruffled dark hair eats cookies from a bag.

'This is Henry. He's my goblin.'

'Your goblin?'

'He does the conventions with me.'

'I'm sorry, what conventions do you do?'

'I dress as a warlock for sci-fi and fantasy conventions. Henry dresses as a goblin,' he breathes impatience. 'We also do children's parties and office events.'

'Oh,' she says. Henry stops in mid-crunch, looking over at her from the sofa. She looks away. 'Do you have a landline?'

'No,' says Henry.

'Yes,' says Riddin.

'Well, yes, but you can't use it. He needs it for work,' Henry says as he eyes her.

'I suppose you could use it once or twice,' Riddin says. 'But you'd have to ask me first. It's possible you could use it very late, say between 1 am and 3 am. That would be all right for you. You're from America, right?'

'Canada. Do you have Internet?'

Henry looks quickly at Riddin. 'Yes. That's my computer,' says Riddin, indicating a desk against the wall. 'But you can't use it. I need it for work.'

She looks from one to the other.

'We have cable,' he continues. 'But we don't want you inviting people around and watching it. If you want to watch it when we're here that's fine, but not if we're not here.'

'OK, well thanks for showing me around,' she says, moving to the front door. Riddin follows her. She turns the door handle and steps outside, turning to see him watching her from the doorway, the black cat in his arms.

She takes a different route back to the station, and on the way she passes an ad that makes her stop still. It is Simon. It is an ad for his concert in Hammersmith. She takes the poster down carefully, rolls it up, and puts it in her bag.

She takes the train to Finsbury Park, and with her paper in one hand, another printed map in the other, she navigates the streets to the ground floor of a low apartment building. She finds the door around the back, off of a green space.

A man with graying hair and a paunch answers the door. He grins when he looks at her.

'I'm Josephine. I spoke to you on the phone about the room you have available.'

'Yes, Josephine, of course,' he says. 'Come in.' He holds the door open for her and she walks past him. She turns to see his eyes raising from her back. 'Please, come this way.'

He leads her down a cramped hallway past mirrored closets that reflect them into infinity. From out of a door a girl wrapped in a bath towel runs giggling across the hall into a bedroom.

'That's the shower,' he says, pointing in the direction she came from. 'And that was Olenka.' He turns and smiles. 'She's from Russia.'

At the next doorway a girl in very short shorts and a shirt falling off one shoulder leans against the doorframe with her arms crossed. She watches Josephine.

'This is Anichka. She's from Kiev.'

Anichka nods and smiles tightly at her. She smiles tightly back.

'This is the room here,' he says, his arm angled to usher her into the plain room a few steps on. She does not enter it, but leans in from the doorway.

'OK. Thanks.'

She looks back at him, and he smiles again after a moment, and leads her on down the corridor to the kitchen. A young blonde girl is at the stovetop and he gives her shoulder a squeeze.

'This is Gabi, from Budapest.'

He sits at the kitchen table, facing her in the doorway, and Gabi slides in next to him. His arm rests loosely on the back of her chair.

'As you can see, we're all pretty friendly in this house.'

'Well, thanks very much for showing me the room,' she says, still standing. There is a moment of nothing. 'I'll have to think about it.'

The smile drops from his mouth, and he rises from the table, leading her back down the corridor to the front door.

She does not turn to look at him when she leaves, but she can feel his eyes on her. As she walks away she turns Siouxsie and the Banshees up loud on her music player, and listens to it all the long way to Battersea. She sits on the second storey of the bus as she crosses the Albert Bridge, looking down the length of it into the Thames below.

She finds the house in a line of lookalikes, white and sagging, collapsing in on itself. She wonders how much longer it will stand. A girl answers the door.

'Hi. I'm Josephine. I'm here about the room.'

'I'm Aibreán. You would have talked to my housemate Gerry. He's doing all the calls, I'm doing all the showing.'

She steps inside the arched entranceway. A tussle of shoes takes up space by the door. She adds her own to it.

'So this is the living room.' The carpet beneath her is bare in patches, exposing scarred wood. Cracks run down from the ceiling. 'We've got cable, and Herm also has video games. I don't know if you're into that.' Aibreán looks at her. 'We don't have a landline, but everyone just uses their mobiles. There's laundry in here …' she leads her into the kitchen. 'We've got a garden,' she peers through the kitchen window into an overgrown wilderness. 'It's great for barbecues in the summer. I'll take you up to the room.'

Something about the house seems cluttered, although it is not overrun with things. It may be the wornness of it, filling the empty spaces, distracting her with texture.

The room Aibreán leads her to has a single bed, a single dresser and a single window. It is all white. She looks it over.

'So there's me, Herm who's from Norway, Gerry who's British, and MJ who's from Australia.'

'Sounds great. When can I move in?'

Aibreán laughs. 'We have had a few people come to see it, so I'll have to let you know in the next couple of days. Is that all right?'

'Sure.' She crosses her fingers behind her back – a gesture she knows is both futile and childish.

That night she dreams of Simon. She is in a house of many rooms, and in each room she goes into she can just see the back of his head, but when she gets closer he is gone. In one room she cannot see him at all and as she talks to a group of her friends they tell her that Simon has just been there, was speaking with them, but has left. She wanders from room to room, but never quite catches him.

Ashley Anderson grew up in a small town in Canada. She studied English, anthropology and psychology at university. She worked in journalism and documentary filmmaking before coming to UEA. After graduation, Ashley plans to finish this novel and begin on her second, which is set in Paris in the 1800s.

Zoë Bolton

Debris

The phone rings. For a moment I think it is you. I sit at the top of the stairs and listen.

'They're staying with me, yeah,' Greta says. 'I think it's better that way. No one wants to be on their own when –'

A pause.

'Luke?' Greta's voice is suddenly higher. 'No … I dunno. But it's been four days now. I mean, that's a long time in a kid's world.'

Another pause. My stomach turns.

'She's not bad, really, considering …'

I imagine the tone of the other person's voice – consolatory, repetitive: *Poor thing. I know, I know.*

'It's just – '

A longer pause. *These things take time. If there's anything at all I can do.*

'Thanks. Yeah, thanks … really.'

Her voice trails off and there's the quick beep of the phone being placed back in the holder.

In the kitchen, Greta is spooning porridge into a deep bowl. Steam curls from the saucepan. Luke watches, open-mouthed, as she bends to unload the washing machine, pulling out the tangled bundle of multi-colours as fast as a magician pulling handkerchiefs from a hat.

'Morning. I've made you some porridge. Eat up, it'll go cold.' She places it on the table, next to a pot of tea. I sit down and fold through the porridge with my spoon. It goes down better than I thought it would, warm and smooth.

'Luke. Would you like to feed the rabbit?' Greta asks.

'Yeah!'

He cups his hands together into a makeshift bowl and Greta gives him some chopped carrot and lettuce leaves. Now he will step outside and feed the rabbit in the hutch by the back door. He will leave food for it in the clamshell you found at the beach the last time we were here. It is one of those rare, intact ones, two halves joined at the base like a castanet. When you found the shell, you scooped it from the sand and held it up to your mouth, puppet-like, singing to Luke who giggled in delight. The wind was strong that day. It pulled our clothes tight against our bodies and whipped sand into our faces. The tide came in close to the wall by the promenade where the wet sand bulged, wobbling like blancmange. A layer of froth had formed just where the tide came in, and bubbles flew through the air. Luke chased them with his finger, ready to pop. You were leaping to catch the foam in both hands, running towards us, drawing your hands open to blow the foam on our faces. Driving back to Greta's, Luke held the shell carefully in one palm, cupping it with the other until we were safely in the house.

Through the patio door, I can see him crouched down chatting to the rabbit, placing the carrot and lettuce in the shell as if it were a little shrine. I see a faint reflection of myself in the glass, frowning, dark patches where my eyes should be. Luke runs up to the door and squashes his face against the glass, leaving a greasy ghost of fingers, nose and mouth. As he pulls away and the steamy circle of his hot breath shrinks against the glass, he stops and meets my eyes. He mimics my frown, sticking out his bottom lip as far as he can, before bringing palm to chin and slowly wiping his face up into a wide-eyed, clown smile, like he's seen you do a thousand times. Something loosens in me.

'You still haven't told him, have you?' Greta's chunky rings knock against the kitchen table as she slides her hand across, placing it on mine.

Silence.

I watch our hands, now clasped together.

He runs off down the garden to his bike. It's a struggle to get the thing going on the grass and he starts circling his legs manically, screwing his face up in concentration.

'I know it's hard, but you have to tell him. There's never going to be a right time.'

'I know.'

She squeezes her fingers around mine. From her grip and the sudden noises coming from her throat, I am sure she is going to cry. I place my free hand over hers and pat it gently, but it feels more like a childhood clapping game of two people placing hand over hand than anything comforting.

I pull my hand away from hers and carry on eating. Part of me wants to be back home, where I can throw myself into the usual clock-watching frenzy.

The porridge has turned stodgy and cold. I swallow and it lodges in my throat.

Back home, Luke will notice things are different.

'He knows his Dad's away a lot for his job, he understands that.' As soon as the words are out, I know how foolish they sound. I have to tell him at some point. I know she is right, that she means well, that this probing is just the honest edge to her goodness. But she has a way of telling me what I already know.

'Ruby. He's a perceptive little kid, you know that.'

I dig my spoon into the porridge and push the bowl away.

The last time we were here, we took the kite up to Badbury Rings and you helped Luke fly it. It was a cold, sunny day, and the red kite slapped about in the wind. I lay back in the grass and when I closed my eyes, there was the kind of red that only happens when you shut your eyes tight against the sun. Greta had made a picnic. We had spread the food out onto a blanket on the top of one of the high, grass-covered ridges. An orange fell from the cool-bag and rolled along the lip of the ridge, settling in a ditch. Later, Greta used the sunshield from the car to grass-sledge down the ridges. *It's an ancient burial ground, not a playground*, I said. But she sat Luke on her lap and slid down, laughing even harder than him. We watched Luke and Greta without talking, other than when you asked for an orange. *None left*, I said and looked down at the ditch where the top half poked out like a setting sun.

Those grass stains on Luke's trousers lingered for two or three washes. Not like the musky scent of you, tucked in shirt collars, clinging to discarded towels – wiped away with one wash.

Luke comes pelting up to the door.
'Mummy! Come outside.'
'Later, sweetheart.' I manage a slow, tight smile.
'Oh, pu-leease.' He looks at Greta and waits. She stands and leaves through the patio door. There's a quick chorus of birdsong and laundry flapping about in the wind, then she slams the door behind her.

The day it happened, we had to stop to get petrol on the way to the hospital. As I waited, the smell of petrol flooding the car, looking out of the window at the starry sky, Greta said something about making a wish on a star for everything to be all right, and I wondered what the hell stars had to do with anything and why people can't just keep quiet, instead of saying something for the sake of it.

They didn't tell us until we got there. They took us into one of those little rooms that are supposed to look welcoming, like a lounge – soft seats, magazines that have never been touched, a tall lamp in the corner. The room smelt of surgical spirit and bleach, like the sleek white floors and corridors in the rest of the building, creeping under the door and settling in the warm, stuffy air.

When they told us, the room seemed to get bigger. It was like groping my way down the stairs in the dark, expecting another step at the bottom but there isn't one.

They brought us tea and I drank mine in big, noisy gulps. Greta brought the cup to her lips and her hands shook so much that the tea spilt and made a little pool in the saucer.

At the hospital chapel I was greeted by a fat man – all puffed out and swollen, like someone had pumped him full of water. His skin was bright red and I thought he might burst at any moment. He had big, swollen hands, too, and when he shook my hand, his grip was too firm and his smile was too jolly.

The room was white and there was a small mahogany table in the corner with a red plastic flower in a glass vase. There was one of those plug-in air fresheners next to the door that made the room smell of lavender. Other than the table and a few paintings on the wall – all of flowers in pastel colours – there was nothing in the room but you, lying there.

    I leaned over and looked at you. I closed my eyes then opened them. I gulped the lavender-scented air.

    The clunk of metal against concrete brings me back to the room. I look out to the garden and see the bike on its side on the patio. Luke underneath it. I'm up and out of my chair. It falls behind me. Outside, the sun hits me. Hot, sharp, white. I see a fleck of deep red on the grey stone by his head.

    'Luke! Are you all right?' My voice comes out high, not like my own. He has already moved from under the bike. Greta is there, pulling a handkerchief from her pocket. She places it on the cut close to his right eye.

    'Let me see,' I say.

    She moves the yellow floral handkerchief to reveal a sticky mess of dirt and blood.

    'You're fine, aren't you, nipper?' she squeezes him close to her. 'It's not deep, it won't need stitches.'

    He starts to cry, quietly at first and then with shaking sobs.

    'Hey, hey ... come on, Luke, you're OK ... where does it hurt?' He points to the cut by his eye. I pinch him gently on the arm, then the leg and tummy, trying to distract him.

    Then I see the shell, almost camouflaged by the patio slabs, broken into bits by his bike. I get down on my knees and frantically gather the pieces.

    'Hey, we can fix it ... no problem.' Parts break off in my hands, leaving a chalky powder over my fingertips. 'We can glue it ... good as new.'

    He wriggles his head into Greta's chest. My hand forms a fist around the pieces, then I uncurl my fingers and they fall to the ground. Luke looks between me and Greta and nestles into her. For a moment, his face is a white blur in the sun, then a cloud passes over and it comes into focus.

    Greta peels his legs from around her waist and passes him to me.

Zoë Bolton was born in Dorset. She taught English in Japan for two years before starting the MA in Creative Writing at UEA, where she received the *Malcolm Bradbury Bursary*. She writes short stories and has begun work on a novel.

Nicholas Brookes

Collision

Two days ago I was commissioned to photograph the CERN institute, accompanied by Norman Fordyce, the renowned author and journalist. The Large Hadron Collider had just been switched on and my newspaper had arranged unprecedented access to the CMS project. We arrived early in the morning at Geneva International airport and were met by one of the chief press officers, Renilde, a tall elegant man with impeccable English who stooped and peered over a clipboard. He drove us in silence through Cessy, a small suburban town. I imagined the epic tunnels with their rushing particles just underneath the seemingly placid streets. I photographed the passing scenes from the car window, more out of boredom than any belief that I would capture a clear picture. The complex's entrance was not far from the centre of town, but once inside, the trim white housing gave way to empty lanes named after famous scientists, and the chatter of cars and school children was replaced by the distant whirring of machines and electric motors. I took many photographs that morning: wide angled shots of empty vistas and metal structures arranged in even avenues like a toy town.

We were led into the tunnel. Norman conducted an interview on a top gantry with one of the maintenance workers. I photographed them, but they stood flatly and paid me no attention. I went and peered onto the hulk of machinery below. The pipeline fed into a grand wheel that rose several storeys high. It looked more like a Victorian steam engine with great cogs and stubs of metal. I brought up my digital camera. As I leant over the balustrade, a sheen of light struck out across the top section of the pipe. There were, of course, no windows, the opening to the overground shut. Neither was there anything odd about the placement of halogens along the undersides of each gantry. The light flickered into the dark tunnel.

'Will we get to go downstairs?' I asked, turning back.

'Of course, in good time. You'll be the first. We promised,' Renilde said.

'I'd really like to photograph down there,' I pointed. 'Now if possible?'

None of the scientific talk had bothered me. Norman had been in a state of excitement during the entire flight from London, yet it was this break of light that had finally intrigued my photographer's eye. I was desperate to go downstairs and inspect the curves and angles of this structure and how the light cast across it. I badgered Renilde. He drew his finger down the clipboard.

'We're scheduled to meet Professor Davies in twenty minutes,' he said.

'More than enough time,' I replied.

He glanced down at his schedule once more.

We went downstairs. Renilde gave a cursory explanation that this was a juncture in the pipeline.

'I'll explain more later in the tour,' he said. Norman looked at me and shrugged his shoulders.

I trailed around the wheel. The scale was even more impressive at the base and looking closely I saw circuit boards and tiny wires over the face of the metal. However, as I crouched and snapped my camera, I saw nothing strange about it. There was the odd kink and bend, an esplanade of screws that caught an interesting perspective, but nothing odder than any other grand piece of machinery. Nothing like the intense stretch of light I had seen from the balcony.

We were led back out of the underground. It was turning into a crisp September morning. The sparseness of the complex was now even more apparent. As my eyes accustomed to the sharp sky, I saw hills on the distant horizon between the gaps in buildings. We were driven to a cheap looking office block, a couple of storeys high with reinforced windows. A couple of shrubs grew in pots by the main entrance. It seemed quaint and sad in comparison to the rest of the complex, so I photographed it. We had to show our passes at the door and it took me a while to untangle mine from the two cameras that also hung around my neck.

'This is where our theorists live,' said Renilde as we followed him up the stairs.

On the second floor there was a long corridor that stretched the width of the building. One side was lined with windows and the other a row of doors marked with the occupants' names. Some of the doors had been left ajar, but most were shut.

'Professor Davies,' Renilde said, 'is one of the few English high-level researchers.' He knocked on a closed door.

Professor Davies had a grey beard flecked with remnants of auburn and his hair ran over the top of his ears. He was slumped over his desk. He turned to us and re-rolled his shirtsleeves back over his elbows. He motioned for us to sit down at a sofa to the back of the office. The three of us: Norman, Renilde and I, squashed in together. I had a little look around while he properly introduced himself and Norman set up his Dictaphone. The shelves were stacked with books, and the desk was overrun with papers.

Norman quizzed the Professor about the theorists' corridor. Apparently they were employed simply to argue with one another about the effects and possible findings of the Collider. The Professor spoke with a great deal of enthusiasm about the Higgs Boson and other such things. I impatiently fingered the crooks and inclinations of my camera. I hoped I would be asked to photograph the room. It was too cramped for me simply to stand up and start snapping. I looked to the window. The blinds were half drawn. A slice of light cut underneath, highlighting a line of dust in the air. The light I had seen at the wheel was something similar; it had been organic. However, its brilliance, its starkness was still nothing like the soft September sunshine.

'What do you think of these claims from that Russian pair?' asked Norman.

There was a moment of silence. You could hear the Dictaphone faintly rolling on.

'You would be talking about Areich and Volveva and their claims of time travel? I think they're optimistic and media hungry. However, there's a possibility that the Collider will form black holes through which we can …'

'Like a piece of light,' I interrupted. All three men looked at me and laughed. It was the first thing I had said since entering the room. I had been quiet all morning, simply content to snap away.

'Sorry?' said the Professor. I noticed his heavy, drawn eyes and jowly chin, as he gave the other two a bemused look.

I continued: 'By mistake or fluke or whatever, just a shard of light somehow, caught and flipped back through a hole.'

'We're talking about miniature black holes, tinier than we can see, open for just a second at the moment of collision,' the Professor said.

'Exactly, just ajar, a slight shard of light.'

The Professor paused for a moment. 'The holes are a slim possibility – we could examine them further, but nothing would be coming or going,' he chuckled to himself. 'I'm certain of that.'

'Why are you so obsessed with this shard of light?' Norman whispered across to me.

I ignored him and addressed the Professor. 'What if I saw a strange glimpse of light that then went away?'

All three men laughed. The Professor spoke again:

'Look, if it's black holes you're interested in, you wouldn't see anything. It would be tiny – reacting deep within the Collider. Certainly nothing on the outside. It was probably a reflected belt buckle or watch face.'

'It was stranger than that. And anyway, if someone was to travel, you're saying they would come into the Collider? Inside it?'

'I'm saying nothing is travelling anywhere. The Russian pair say that with this understanding we could manipulate doorways.'

'A doorway ajar – a shard of light.'

They laughed again.

'You've been reading too much science fiction, watching too much *Star Trek*,' said Renilde.

'I don't read at all,' I said turning to him.

'That's the problem then,' said Norman.

'It's possible, I guess. Everything is possible,' said the Professor.

'Let me show you then.' I leaned forward.

'We have sensors and readings all down the line – I'd already know if something had occurred.'

Collision

'But you're looking inside the pipe,' I said. The Professor looked me in the eye, seemed to tighten the loose skin around his jaw. 'Just walk with me.'

I can't say whether it was something I said or simply my desperate attitude that swayed the Professor, but he eventually agreed to accompany me down the tunnel. He went to arrange permission, while Renilde led us to a small room close to the tunnel entrance. It was supposed to be lunchtime on Renilde's schedule. Norman and I drank tea out of polystyrene cups.

'You do know the tunnel goes on for seventeen miles? I'm sure as hell not walking down it for a bit of light,' Norman said.

Professor Davies returned and Renilde led Norman away. The Professor and I entered the tunnel at the same place as before. We went past the juncture that I had photographed earlier. I stood for a moment at the entrance where the gantries gave way and the tunnel walls arched and enclosed around the orange piping. As we walked down the tunnel there was the faintest echo of our footsteps against the concrete floor. We didn't speak much. Occasionally, the Professor's two-way radio spat out a snatch of distortion, a clipped, garbled message. I photographed everything: signs, doorways, odd angles of metal. I had left my digital behind, more content with my old Nikon; the weight easier, the action more fluent. I snapped without ever stopping to set up the frame. I used an entire reel of film. I sharply fitted a new roll into the camera.

'Very flash,' said the Professor.

It was after about an hour of walking that we saw it.

'There,' I said and pointed to a break of intense light at the top of the pipe. It flashed out sharply, jutting out into space rather than following the easy contour of the pipe. I felt assured; it was fresh and organic next to the fluorescent orange and gun metal grey of the tunnel. I didn't wait to gauge the Professor's reaction and immediately set about taking pictures. I darted around, viewing and snapping from every angle. I crouched up close. I zoomed in, right up to my camera's limits. I saw what looked like bacteria squirming under a microscope. Fat yellow globs swam, darted and merged across a garish background. I shot quickly, ignoring the strong glare. Then the light adjusted and formed a crude facial shape like that of the moon. I took a picture and it moved again. It formed a jowly chin, then an elegant nose, then old eyes, and finally, just for a second, I swear I saw my own reflection.

My camera whirred and ran out of film. I ejected the dead canister and let it cannon to the floor. I twisted a new one from my strap, but in the excitement, with my eyes still trained on the moving light I dropped it. It rattled on the concrete. The light intensified. I reeled back from the viewfinder. The light disappeared, then returned smaller and winked away once more. I turned to face the Professor. He was searching along the line of halogens. He looked at me, his mouth open, his chin drooped. He swung his watch in the space between us, hoping to recapture a slice of light. He dropped his arm. He shook his head, then pointed towards me, towards my chest, where the dead weight of my camera hung. I fitted the cap back over the lens.

'Just wait 'till the film develops,' I said.

Nicholas Brookes was born in 1984 and grew up in South London. He writes fictional narratives set around real life events. His novel, *Pollination*, is centred around the London July 7th bombings. He is also working on a book of linked postmodern stories entitled *The Archivist*.

Dea Brovig

The Best Room
An extract from a novel

It was on a blue-eyed Saturday afternoon in midsummer that Hans first kissed Nina outside the toilets of the bus depot.

He was waiting for her when she tripped out of the cubicle, a square of tissue stuck to the heel of her tennis shoe. She froze when she saw him. In the car park, as greasy mists from the mobile kitchen settled over her skin like clingfilm, Nina blinked at the stripe of Hans's smile. He lifted his hands to her shoulders and pulled her close, his chapped lips gathering into a pucker and gluing shut her mouth. Hard, soft. Wet, rough. Her stomach churned; the bubbles danced along her throat. Between her ears. She was all fizz. It felt like laughing.

That evening, Pastor Seip was coming for supper and Nina had instructions from her mother not to be late. While Hans raced his moped against the other boys', zipping and skidding along the dirt, she checked her watch, noting uneasily that she had just missed another ferry. She looked up and tried to catch his eye but he was absorbed by the business of winning. It couldn't hurt to wait a few minutes more. Nina picked a chip from a paper plate in her lap and bit it in half. A dollop of Thousand Island dressing dribbled onto her T-shirt as Hans took his fourth victory of the day.

When it could no longer be avoided, she rose to her feet. Hans's moped changed course and started speeding towards her. She looked at her shoes, at her hands. A crust of dirt under one fingernail suddenly demanded her urgent attention.

'Are you leaving?' Hans asked as he jerked to a stop in front of her.

She glanced up as if surprised to see him. 'Ferry goes in five minutes,' she said.

'Want to go for a ride?'

'I have to leave,' Nina said. 'Pastor Seip's coming for dinner.'

Hans crossed his eyes and she felt a snort of laughter shoot up her nose like soda pop.

'OK, well, see you tomorrow at church,' he said.

Nina launched into a jog down the high street, overtaking one white timber building after another. At the bottom of the hill, the fjord spread out like the night sky, the ripples of water twinkling in the light. The ferry was already docked at the Longpier. She hopped onto its deck and made her way to the stern. Standing with her back to the other passengers, she listened to the engine's tick above the slop of the waves. Sharp, clean bursts of salt air splashed her face. The captain pushed the boat away from land and they began to sway up the fjord.

As they passed, Nina counted the rocks that bubbled up from the deep and lurked close to the surface like aspiring icebergs, and she tried to dismiss the creeping worry that tiptoed up and down her spine. She glanced at her watch and her stomach pinched. What time was Pastor Seip meant to arrive? She hoped her father would be in a fit state when she got home. At breakfast that morning, his breath had been foul with the onions he chewed to mask the stink of the moonshine. Nina knew all about the distillery he kept hidden in the outhouse; he must have visited it every night that week. She peered over the side of the ferry at the stripe painted by the propeller and thought of Hans's smile. She closed her eyes, but it dissolved in the darkness.

At the public dock, Nina scrambled to land and retrieved her bicycle from where she'd left it behind an oak. The springs of the saddle dug into her as she set off along the zigzag of the coastline. She took the turns without braking, shooting past lonely farmhouses sharp as redcurrants against the grey mountain. The wind was picking up. It greased her hair flat and worked the fjord up into short, fast waves. Nina redoubled her efforts, screwing tighter the muscles in her calves. Her wheels rattled and sprayed dirty fans behind her. Under her breath, she prayed that Pastor Seip would be late.

By the time she reached the farmhouse, her ears were buzzing. She hurried inside. Her mother was in the kitchen, apron flapping at the knees as she pivoted between the oven and her pots. Beside her, Nina's father clutched the counter and belted out instructions.

'That goddamned fish has to go in *now*!'

Nina hurried over to the sink to wash her hands.

'You're late,' her mother said.

'Where have you been?' Her father spoke to her with a snap in his voice. His eyes were tinged with blood.

'The ferry didn't come,' Nina said.

'Pastor Seip will be here any minute.' Johann looked at Nina as though it were all her fault. 'Clean yourself up and get going,' he said and turned back to Dagny's cooking.

After changing into her Sunday dress, Nina raced down the stairs and began wiping the dinner table.

'The potatoes! The potatoes!' her father hooted from the kitchen as she carried through a cloth still warm from the clothesline and shook it over the polished wood.

The good plates were stacked in a high cabinet. Nina climbed onto a chair to retrieve them.

'The butter! It's burning!'

A layer of dust had settled on the top dish like mould. She quickly rubbed it off with the hem of her dress and set a place at the head of the table for Pastor Seip.

She saw him through the window as he stepped through the gate.

'He's here!' she called.

Nina's warning was met with the sound of shuffling feet as her parents scurried out to the hallway. They checked their reflection in the mirror, smoothing hair and wiping foreheads on shirtsleeves and apron tails. Dagny opened the door just as the minister's fist was poised to knock.

Supper was, by all accounts, a success. Pastor Seip doused his potatoes in melted butter that floated on his plate like an oil spill. He polished off the pollack he had been served and helped himself to seconds.

'Very nice,' he muttered afterwards, suppressing a burp behind his knuckles.

'We'll take coffee and cake in the Best Room,' Dagny said. Her face was as solemn as a sermon. She rose from the table and led the way across the hall to the pride of the house.

It was the first time they had used the Best Room since Easter, although Nina had helped her mother dust its cracks and corners that morning. Now, sitting opposite Pastor Seip on a low-slung bench, she felt the chill that the room imparted to all special occasions. The pine walls were stained a midnight blue that sucked the warmth right out of the air. Lace curtains filtered the sunlight, scattering it over the furniture like shards of glass.

Pastor Seip's stomach folded neatly over his thighs as he leaned forward for his coffee cup. Nina watched its progress to his lips, thinking how unfair it was that she was not allowed one herself.

'I hear the catch has been meagre,' Pastor Seip said to Johann and took a sharp slurp from his dainty cup.

The china had been a wedding gift from Dagny's brother, Olav, a sea captain whose merchant ship had been lost in the North Pacific. Nina had been a baby when it happened. Sometimes, when she had the farmhouse to herself, Nina would sneak into the Best Room and flip the lock of the cupboard to rescue a cup from the top shelf, cradling it in her hands. She would trace a fingertip around the outline of a gold leaf on a black sea and try to imagine where it had come from.

'It's on account of the water,' her father said.

'It's a matter of vigilance,' said Pastor Seip.

'It's too warm,' said Johann. 'The shrimp are not to be found.'

Pastor Seip fixed him with a meaningful glare. '"Be sober,"' he said, '"be vigilant, for your adversary the devil, as a hungry lion, walketh about seeking whom he may devour."'

'More coffee?' Dagny said.

'Keeping one's eyes open,' said Pastor Seip. 'That's the point.' Johann shifted in his chair and a creak filled the room. The minister looked at Nina for the first time all evening. 'Amazing what we see, if we only open our eyes.' His gaze fell like an anchor and she stifled the urge to squirm out of its way. She thought of Hans's eyes, how he'd shut them tight when he kissed her. She watched as Pastor Seip deposited a cube of cake on his tongue.

'Another slice?' Dagny said.

'No, no.' He mashed the crumbs on his plate with his finger and slipped it between wet lips. 'I have other duties this evening.' Pastor Seip stood up and brushed his palms on his trousers. 'Thank you for the fish. It was just as my mother used to make it, which is the best way I know.'

At the front door, he took his hat and turned again to Nina. 'Soon we'll have to start preparing for your confirmation,' he said.

Nina nodded at her feet.

'Yes, of course,' said Dagny.

He pulled his hat down on his slippery-smooth head. 'An important time in every young woman's life.' Pastor Seip bent forward at the hips, bringing his face level with Nina's. He blinked. His breath smelled of coffee. 'Remember,' he said, 'you must pray, and you must work. It is always possible, I believe, to work harder.'

He straightened up and stepped into the sun. He did not look over his shoulder as he walked through the yard towards the fjord. When Nina turned, her father was standing rigid in the doorway of the Best Room, icicle pale against the midnight blue walls. He stared blankly at her. Without a word, he spun on his heel, retreating back into the darkness of the room. He pushed the door shut behind him.

Nina and Dagny washed the dishes in silence. For a long time after Pastor Seip had left, Johann sat alone in the Best Room. The groan of floorboards and the bang of the back door announced his escape. Nina watched her father through the kitchen window, striding towards the outhouse. She knew they wouldn't see him again that evening.

'I'll have to dig up some more onions,' Dagny said. She added a chopped bulb to the fish bones in her pot.

Later that night, when Nina had already been asleep for several hours, a crash outside jolted her awake. She opened her eyes but the room was black as water. Rain hammered the roof, spilling through her window and gathering in a puddle on the floor, while the furious wind rushed in and pounded her about the head. She stumbled across her bedroom to close the window but as she grabbed the latch, another

Dea Brovig

crash made her peer over the sill.

There was darkness, only darkness, then thunder and a shiver of electricity. Nina saw him for just a moment and he was gone.

Another thunder shock, a split of white lightning. Johann was still there, now further down the yard, approaching the pier. She saw him stumble. Darkness. A howl that may have been the wind.

With each further illumination, she measured her father's progress. *Crack!* He kneeled beside the *Freya*. *Crack!* He lurched from land to deck. *Crack!* The trawler pulled away from the pier. The sea reared to meet the wind, hurling the boat from one peak to another. The *Freya* was shrinking. Then she was gone. Nina pulled her window shut.

She crept through the darkness back into bed. The quilt settled over her body like a snowdrift. Curling her knees to her chest, Nina forced herself to think of Hans, to remember his breath spilling onto her tongue. The glass rattled in the window frame. She pressed her lips against the back of her hand.

Dea Brovig moved to England from her native Norway in 1994. She worked in publishing in London from 2000 to 2008. In October 2009, her story 'Ania's Wake' will appear in Tindal Street Press's *Roads Ahead* anthology, edited by Catherine O'Flynn. She is currently working on a novel.

Tyona Campbell

Saw Him

There is a naked man lying on my bed, reading this morning's copy of *The Financial Times*. His body is plump in the way of someone who has been formerly muscular. He has crumpled the bed sheets, nestling his weight onto my clean pillows. He turns his face to me and smiles, displaying young yet worn out features and a set of perfectly straight, whitish teeth. It does not startle me that he is there, with nothing but a newspaper to provide decency. We do not say a word to each other.

I live in a house full of drop-outs, part-time students and half-way travellers so there are always people milling around. Many of the rooms are being sub-let and it is difficult to keep track of who is who in such an elongated and forgotten house: an unknown naked man lying on someone's bed is nothing out of the ordinary. I can not be bothered to ask him to leave, so go downstairs and sleep on the cigarette-butt-infested sofa.

For weeks after the first encounter I did not see him, but there is the occasional clue that suggests that he has been around. I find a single man's sock or an old newspaper hidden in my bedroom. I lock the door but somehow his damn things find a way in.

Late one Sunday night he turns up dressed in a creased black suit. His shoes are scuffed, but shine on the top.

'I was wondering if you would like to go out to dinner?' He asks in a smooth voice.

'What?' I lean up against the wall and cross my arms.

'Please don't be alarmed, Mimi, I just want to take you out. Make up for scaring you the other night.' It occurs to me that he knows my nickname and says it with such conviction that it feels like he has known it for some time.

'Who the fuck are you?' I can feel adrenaline throbbing in my ear.

'My name is Ban. Look, I know this is going to sound crazy Mimi, but I've seen you around and it's weird, but I have made up my mind, and you have to be in my life.' We sit on the rickety bed, our eyes mirroring each other as we both try to figure out each other's next move. I grab a couple of chipped glasses from my chest of drawers and a bottle of cheap vodka and pour us a drink. The vodka licks my throat with fire and I quickly chase it down with another swig.

'Ban, I have no idea who you are or where you're from. This whole thing seems like bullshit ...' I could feel him searching my face. 'But there is something about you. Something different. You're a pretty fucking weird kettle of fish.' I swallow another mouthful of vodka and think how I haven't been on a date for months and Ban sort of intrigues me. 'Yeah, I'll go out for dinner with you. Keep it simple, I don't like anything fancy.'

His cold face immediately lights up like a pinball machine; bright colours flashing in his eyes. 'Let's go early next week.' Once I have agreed, he slides away like the shadow of a passing car; the door hardly seems to open or close. I find it difficult to sleep that night.

The next time I see Ban is in an Italian restaurant a couple of tube stops from where I live; north of Wembley on the Bakerloo line. He left a screwed up note on my bed a few days previously explaining where the place was. Underlined in block capitals it states that I was, 'NOT TO BE LATE'. The restaurant walls are covered in Italian newspaper cuttings that are glazed in cooking fat. Ban is seated in a faux leather red booth in the back corner, surrounded by low candlelight. As I walk up to the table, he rises to his feet and gives me a fleeting bow. He looks incredibly dapper. His white shirt is starched and correctly ironed with military precision. He is far more sprucely dressed than I had seen him before. I am wearing a hip-hugging scarlet dress, with a slit running up my thigh. It accentuates my better features; well at least that's what I hope.

'You look beautiful, Mimi. Like something out of a classic black and white film. Truly stunning,' he whispers, bending his head towards the table. My hands feel jittery.

'Thank you Ban, you look good yourself.' His skin glows like the flesh of an apricot in the candlelight. 'Hey, why the whispering?' I notice two waiters keep staring at him.

'No real reason. I went to school with the man over there.' He points at a table near the window. 'I just don't want him to see me or speak to me. You know the type. The ones that mean nothing to you.' His voice is almost inaudible.

'Yeah, I know what you mean.' We nod.

For nearly ten minutes the conversation is mute. Ban's eyes are transfixed on the guy near the window. I start to make plans on which dish I want to order. I hadn't been out for dinner in a long time.

'Do you like fish, Ban?' He doesn't answer. 'Ban, do you like seafood, fish, things like that?' I can hear his fingers tapping under the table and I notice him biting the skin around his lips. 'I bet you're the sort of man that will try something new?'

He pretends not to notice me and then exhales through his nose with a sense of knowingness. I still try to show interest and even push myself to flirt, but his cold behaviour forces me to react. I swing the laminated menu at him, knocking over a couple of candles causing hot wax to pour over his trousers. Ban immediately leaps up like an overwound tin toy.

'Fuck, you're crazy!' Surrounding customers turn and stare and the waiters chuckle amongst themselves. I grab my coat, look Ban straight in the eyes and leave. This is the end of our first date.

Things did get better. We stayed at my house from then on and watched nostalgic films together, played board games and ordered takeaways which Ban always paid for. He felt guilty about his attitude in the restaurant and later explained that he didn't feel himself that night; the guy near the window had bullied him at school. Ban felt this old acquaintance would not have understood why a girl like me was on a date with him. I was comforted by the trust he placed in me. We stayed up until dawn most nights talking about everything and anything. We had so much in common and agreed with each other, entirely. We never went to his flat. Ban liked the bustling of people and the feeling that more was going on than in fact really was.

At midnight Ban would sometimes take me for a walk around Stonebridge Park. It was always closed when we got there but we liked to view the park from the iron fencing. It made us feel safe. Ban would anxiously kiss me inbetween the street lamps, in the pockets of darkness. He would encompass my body with his long coat and it felt like we were moulding into each other. The romance had whittled into me like a woodworm. In this dismal, restless city, Ban and I had found each other.

'Do you think I'll ever meet your parents?' I ask. We are languidly sprawled across the bed. Ban is naked but for a pair of moth-eaten bed socks. He is engrossed in a cryptic crossword.
'I don't have any parents.'
'I know you have parents, I've heard you talk about them. We have been together for months now and I haven't even met one of your friends.'
'Can we not talk about this, Mimi? You should understand me.' I was learning when to stop.
One thing that continued to confuse me is that we had never made love. Not even close to it. He would lie on my bed for hours and pleasure himself. It may sound ridiculous but I would take comfort from this. I gained satisfaction from seeing him read, sleep and his moments of silence. I was lost. Lost in Ban.
'Mimi, tell me why I can't meet your parents?' His tone is sarcastic.
'You know why you can't meet them.' My family are a faded memory and I wanted them to stay that way. 'Sometimes you are really spiteful, Ban. Sometimes I wish you had never walked in here.' I grab my keys and coat. 'I'm going out and when I come back I don't want you to be here.'
'Sit down, Mimi, relax. You can't go out.' He speaks with rhythmical ease like a ticking clock.
'Who the hell are you to tell me what I can do?'
'You can try and leave Mimi, but nothing will happen. Only I can tell you when to go or when to come back.' Ban folds down his newspaper and sits upright. 'You are no one, Mimi.' Uncontrollably I slump myself onto the dirty floor and grip my hands around my waist.
'Who are you, Ban? What are you? Why the fuck did you come here?' Tears instantly emerge and then melt into my skin. He is calculating his words.
'This is my bedroom, Mimi. I made you come here.' His voice claws

into my ears and like a freshly shot pigeon my body flinches and stiffens. 'And I can also make you go away.' Ban turns his face from me, unfolds the newspaper and smoothly carries on with the crossword.

'Ban, look at me, why the fuck won't you look at me?'

A sharp tainted grin appears on his face. He does not answer.

'Ban, I don't understand. What is going on? I need you.'

I drag myself over to the bed and scream. He does not hear me. I hit the bed with my fists. He does not move.

As I inhale I can taste blood rasping in my throat like gritty molasses. I dig my fingers into his knees as venom punctures my gut. The lights flash, and something flashes inside my head. I faint.

Weeks have now passed and I keep myself in this closed bedroom. No one comes to visit and I have begun to question if they had ever noticed me before I met Ban. He has moved his belongings in and uprooted his life into mine. The room is cluttered with piles of musty newspapers and a scattering of unwashed clothes.

I am frail. My palms have turned a deep shade of purple and I keep sweating poisoned seeds. I look in the mirror and can see that my eyes are splintered with burst blood vessels and encrusted around my mouth are the remnants of pink lipstick and saliva.

I hope that the door will open and this dank air will pour out, but instead there is the smell of festering dry rot which I can see on the gnawed floorboards. My curtains are torn and there is a flowerless vase which has smashed, producing hundreds of glass arrows. The moon hanging at the window makes them glitter like wet tarmac. A stale masculine odour has overpowered my senses; I know this isn't my domain any more.

Ban has wallpapered my cranium in a sick floral print, gluing his thoughts into my own. I watch his naked flesh recoil into our sheets and in my foul-mouthed and restless state I see his gluttonous dreams begin. I have been left to float alone.

Occasionally, Ban will catch my eye and gives me a mawkish wink. I think he knows only I can see him.

Tyona Campbell was born in 1984 and lives in Suffolk. She studied English Literature and Creative Writing at Aberystwyth University in Wales before coming to UEA.

Gillian Daly

Scrap

Scrap is an extract from a longer piece entitled The Wash

The police came in the morning to search the Wash for her. It was Sunday, and the church bells were ringing across the fields where in the week the gypsies worked the terraces. I watched from the yard, past the barbed wire fence, as the churchgoers pulled their cars over to let the blue sirens pass. King was still sleeping in the caravan and the yard was empty except for the greyhounds yelping in the coop.

King was a scrap man. The yard and all the scrap belonged to his grandfather who had the stroke and went to live in the care home. There were cars stripped down and stacks of logs. The grandfather loved the greyhounds and King wouldn't sell them. He wouldn't race them neither. He kept them in the coop that was made for chickens. When they weren't yelping, they stood on their long legs, with their long necks, and turned their heads at me snootily.

Them dogs don't like me, I told King once, when he was fixing up the mesh, but he didn't listen.

The greyhounds yelped so loud after the blue lights went past that King came out the caravan. He stood on the step, his hand shielding away the sun and you could see he had the jitters. He'd been turning on the mattress all night. He went back inside and when he came out again he was wearing his jeans. He didn't say anything and he didn't look at me neither as he crossed the yard. He went into the workshop and shut the doors behind him. You could tell he was working on the scrap because of the banging that started.

I went over to the fence to see along the main road. The police cars had stopped by the river banks but the blue lights were still flashing. Then the lights stopped and it was too far away for you to see anything. I kept changing my mind about going down there then I was set on it. I washed from the drum where the rainwater had collected. There wasn't much left because of the hot weather. It was so dark inside the drum that even when you leaned in to find the water you couldn't see your face.

When I was done washing, I walked along the edge of the road to the river. The mud had turned dusty in the heat. You could smell the strawberries rotting early in the fields. The gypsy vans were parked on the scrub. There were fires smoking and lines of washing strung up between the trees. Some of the gypsies were walking towards the river. One of the churchgoers had stopped his car beneath the bank and was struggling up the grassy rise in his suit.

The churchgoers didn't like the gypsies who came each year for the picking season. They were always trying to get the council to move them on. They didn't like King and me neither. Sometimes, they came rattling at the gates of the yard with their talk of salvation. They looked at King when they read from their testaments. King liked to put on a show for them. One time, when I was fourteen and just come to the yard, he ran his hand up my dress and kissed me so hard I lost my balance when he let go.

The bank was so high that it dropped a shadow over the road before I got there. I climbed past the cars and stood with the gypsies. Two police in uniforms were walking along the river towards the Wash. A diver was putting his tank on.

Local woman, one of the gypsies said, two days missing.

There were more police in suits talking with a man. He was well done up, in the circumstances, with a jumper, a tie and a proper pair of black shoes. I wondered if he was a teacher, like she was. He waved his hands about as the police talked. For a moment, when he turned around, you might have thought he was pointing at the scrap yard. Further along the bank, the police in uniforms were getting smaller. You couldn't look that way for long. Out there, where the river met the Wash, the sun was blinding.

I knew the scrap yard and the Wash long before I knew King. It was my father who taught me about them both. He took me out on the Wash the first time when I was seven. He gave me a bucket for my birthday so I could help with the collecting. It stayed outside the back door for two days while the rain slanted across the fields. When the rain stopped, my father got the rake from the shed while I put my wellies on. The potholes were full with water and our feet plunged through them as we walked up the row. When we passed the houses, the dyke kept on running to the scrap yard. The yard looked magical after the rain. The parts of things were spread out across the mud: broken chairs, car doors, tyres piled in lop-sided towers. Water dripped down the stacks of cars and made them shine.

As we passed the yard the dogs sniffed along the fence. You could still hear them whining when we got further up the road. We climbed the bank and looked back the way we'd come. It was the first time I'd seen the world from up there. The fields and the houses were laid out beneath. As far away as you could see were the low buildings of the cannery. A thin line of steam came out the roof and brought the vegetable smell.

I followed my father along the bank, past the swing bridge and the lighthouse, until we came to the marsh. We stopped on the edge of it. The wind pushed me back as I looked at the mud flats. It was the patterns, the ridges and swirls, that caught your eye. My father nodded towards the mud.

A halfway place, he said, not land and not sea neither.

The wind gusted and I moved behind my father's legs but I kept looking at the patterns. The leftovers of the water filled the dips.

The Wash is always changing, my father said, that's what you need to remember.

The wind made his breath short.

You can come here a thousand times but you'll never see it the same as it is right now.

We watched the patterns from far away, then I watched them pass beneath as I followed my father's feet across the mud. He stopped part way out and pointed down at some holes the size of pencil pricks. I knew what lay underneath. I'd seen my father boil the cockles in a pan and sell them with vinegar at market. I knelt beside him on the mud and his body kept the wind from me. He showed me how to rake the mud over until the shells began to show. We moved slowly out, filling our buckets, the air cold and salty to the skin. I watched the waders as we worked tottering about on their skinny legs. There was no sound out there but the wind blowing past your ears.

When we'd nearly filled our buckets my father stood and pulled his jacket tight. He looked out to sea where the sky was darker. The birds were lifting in a great cloud. He said it was time for going home and hurried me across the mud. When we reached the marsh, I turned back to look. The Wash was already changing just like my father said it would. Shadows smoothed the patterns in the mud away.

My father carried both buckets and we walked back slower than we came. We stopped part way along the bank and sat on the grass a while. The wetness seeped through my jeans as my father peeled an orange and passed half to me. He sucked the juice from his half and threw the skin into the river. Then he lay back, his big feet pointing up to the sky. I threw my leftovers after his and lay back as well. The sky was a blur of pink and the salt air made you yawn. I turned onto my elbows and looked down the bank. The square of the scrap yard was sitting halfway home. A small fire was burning. The black smoke blew over the caravan and made the sky look redder.

I thought about the parts of things that were laid out on the dirt that morning. I thought about the old man who sometimes sat outside the caravan smoking a pipe in his foldaway chair. Then I thought about the vans with cranes on the back that brought the cars late at night. I turned over and asked my father what the yard was for. He took a while to answer.

It's where things go, he said, when nobody wants them any more.

I waited by the river until the police in uniforms disappeared behind the swing bridge then I went back down the bank. The sun was right up and burning my shoulders as I walked along the road past the gypsy vans. I kept the key for the yard around my neck on the string King gave me. When I got back there, I shut the gates tight behind me and did the chain up. When you were in the yard it was like everything outside was divided off and faraway. I went over to the workshop and looked through the gap in the door. King was still there but he wasn't working any more.

He was sitting on the chair beside a pile of scrap with his head down. King didn't like me going in the workshop. As well as the scrap, the walls were lined with books that belonged to his grandfather who had the stroke.

I knew King had read the books because sometimes at night when we lay on the mattress he said bits of them to me. It made me laugh hearing all them high things coming from him. He'd cut a skylight in the roof of the van and he pulled the plastic back on warm nights so you could see the stars up there.

Where'd you go? he asked me once when we were looking up at the sky.
What? I said.
Where'd you go if you could go anywhere?

I turned on my side and reached my arm over King. I could feel his ribs beneath my fingers as I pressed against him. His skin was warm on my face. Then there was the smell of him. I never knew anyone who smelt like King. There was petrol and sweat, kelp from the Wash, the liquorice he was always chewing. I couldn't think of nowhere else.

I watched King sitting on his chair in the workshop, his back rising and falling as he breathed, but I couldn't make myself go in. I tried not to look towards the river as I walked back across the yard. I kept seeing the police in uniforms halfway out to the Wash and peering down the bank for a glimpse of her. The sun was making every part of me run with sweat. I went to the front end of the caravan and sat with my back against it where the sun didn't reach. All you could see that way were the empty fields. There was no steam coming from the cannery. The greyhounds were quiet and a strange stillness had come over everything. I pulled my knees up and waited.

Gillian Daly is a former barrister. Her short fiction has appeared in *Mslexia* and been shortlisted for the Asham Award.

Jonathan Gibbs

Ed

Perhaps, if I'm honest, I always had it in the back of my mind to write something about Randall one day. What crystallised the thought, though, was having Ed Hitchcock sat in my living room, interviewing me for his biography.

To give him his due, Ed wasn't the first vulture to descend, but still Randall was less than six months dead when Justine called me from New York to say that Ed had been in touch and wanted to write a book. There had already been two cut-and-paste jobs rushed out since Randall's death, and it was obvious that a proper book would need to be written at some point.

It was hardly surprising that Ed put himself forward – he always liked to give the impression that he had discovered Randall – but he must have known he wouldn't be top of anyone's list but his own. We had all always considered him a laughing stock, a classically up-his-own-arse journalist who thought that chucking a bunch of Derrida quotes at a canvas gave you the right to stand next to it and take all the credit, and who sincerely believed that the highest form of literature is the catalogue essay.

'What I reckon,' Randall said to me once, 'is that, deep down, in his dirty little unsubbed heart of hearts, he actually thinks it's him that makes the art. That, before he opens his laptop and spills his *earth-shattering* thoughts into it, it doesn't exist.'

So what Justine and I decided, as trustees of the estate, was that we'd talk to Ed, but that it wouldn't be an authorised biography.

Which is how, one day last year, I came to be welcoming him into my home.

There he stood, on the doorstep, with this meaningful look on his face and a bottle of whisky in his hand. He held it out, then said, 'Fuck it', and leaned in to give me a hug. I'd never hugged the man in my life. It's a horrible thing, being hugged by someone you don't want to be hugged by. You flinch, and they feel you do it, but they've still got to go through with the gesture.

The whisky was good, at least. Caol Ila, I think. He put it down on the table, next to his Dictaphone – a pointed juxtaposition, but I didn't bite. I said why don't we start with a cup of tea and see how we go. I left him looking at the stuff on the walls and went into the kitchen. Let him look, I thought. I'd removed the two Randalls from the room before he came round – a 'Sunshines' portrait of Isabella Blow and a maquette of the Chrome Bionic Duck – replacing them with the most banal things I could lay my hands on – a Martin Parr and a Matthew Collings target.

'So, Ed, how are we going to do this?' I said, once we were settled.

'Look, Vincent, first of all, can I just say how grateful I am to you for speaking to me like this. I know we've had our differences, but the way I see it, this isn't about me, or you, it's about Randall. And I think it's *crucial* that we – all of us – get it all on record now, everything we can remember, before we all cop it' – he picked up his teacup and raised an ironical eyebrow – 'or go ga-ga.'

I nodded, but all I could think was what a conniving git he was, with his crisp white shirt, its collars stiff as jet plane wings, and his chunky-framed glasses. Leaning back in my Jasper Morrison chair, one leg crossed over the other, as if he owned the place.

Compare this, if you will, to the jittery arriviste who turned up at the first warehouse show, back in 1991. He was always hanging around the place, pretending to look at the art, but really snatching peeks at the artists. 'We've got ourselves a groupie,' someone said, and after that it was impossible to take him seriously.

So, yes, the articles he wrote about that show did have a positive impact, and yes, he did continue to write consistently good things about us. The problem was, he clearly thought this meant we had to like him back. No chance of that. We tolerated him, for his good offices, but also as a kind of hapless court jester, who could always be relied upon for not being in on the joke. The joke, more often that not, being him.

Although he revered Randall above all, he did his best to ingratiate himself with the others. With me, it was different. I wasn't an artist – I was a philistine from the City, a pin-striped and moneyed oik with less artistic sensibility than he had in his little toe. And yet somehow I had come to a position of influence in Randall's circle, that he no doubt considered his by right, or at least merit. This long-standing resentment, glazed over with a smarmy faux-chumminess, is what made the circumstances of this interview so amusing to me.

'In a way you're the most important name on my list,' he said, leaning forward, and tapping his finger on my coffee table. 'You have this totally unique perspective on, well, everything. You knew him better than almost anyone. You weren't an artist, you weren't competition. You weren't, you know, a *critic*' – he waggled his head, and did the quotation mark thing with his fingers 'You were his *friend*.'

'So it's like my personal view of Randall you want,' I said, 'The Randall no one else saw.'

'Yes, exactly.'

'The off-duty Randall.'

'Exactly that. Yes, thank you. The *off-duty* Randall.'

'Like, for instance,' I went on, offering him a biscuit, 'the time we sent you out to buy heroin because Randall was having a really bad acid experience?'

He sat there, frozen, his mouth still smiling bravely on, the shock only registering in his eyes. Then, from somewhere, he managed to dredge up a laugh of sorts.

'Christ. I'd forgotten about that. That was *insane*. Hmm ... will that go in? In all honesty, Vincent, I don't think so. But yes, that's exactly the *kind of thing* I'm after.' He laughed again and put his hand through his hair. 'Bloody hell, what was that bloke's name? He was a nutter.'

I give him my best icicle smile.

'I think we told you to ask for Mr Squiffy.'

'Fuck me, yes. That was quite a night.'

Quite a night. Yes, indeed.

LSD was clearly not my drug of choice. I worked for a reputable

Jonathan Gibbs

investment bank after all; I'd have been laughed off the premises if they'd found out I'd taken a hippie drug like acid. Nevertheless, I humoured Randall every so often, when he wanted to really go off on one.

This particular time, we just spent the day walking around Stokey. It was one of those warm spring days that are almost better than summer. We ended up back at Randall's, sat out on the flat roof of the bay window, easing ourselves into the comedown with fruit tea and the odd joint. Then we saw Ed coming along the street. He was going out with a girl who lived nearby, but I suspect he used to detour via Randall's place deliberately, on the off-chance. As soon as he saw him, Randall slid down in his chair, put his hands over his face and started groaning.

Ed stopped below us.

'Hey, how you doing?' he called up.

'I'm fucked,' Randall said to me through his hands, in a low comic rumble. 'I'm having a *really bad trip*.'

I played along.

'Hi, Ed. Well, not so good, actually. Randall's ... well, we're tripping our tits off, and he's going through a bit of a bad patch.' I reached down and rubbed Randall on the back. He moaned in response.

'Christ,' said Ed. 'Is there anything I can do?'

'Heroin,' Randall mumbled.

Then, louder, sounding like a grouchy infant, '*Heroin*.'

I shushed him, trying to keep myself from giggling.

I crawled to the edge of the roof.

'Look, Ed,' I said. ('Skag ... ska-aa-ag,' Randall was whimpering behind me.) 'We could really do with a bit of heroin.' ('Squirrels. The fucking *squirrels*.') 'For him to smoke, you know. Just to bring him down gently.'

'Right. Right. Heroin. And you want me to ...'

Randall kicked my foot and whispered, 'Send him to Mr Squiffy.'

I had no idea who this was supposed to be.

'Hang on a sec,' I said to Ed, and turned round. 'Who?' I mouthed back at Randall.

'*Si*. Send him to Si.' He was peeking out between his fingers, showing the glint of a smile. 'You know, *Mr Squiffy*.'

So we gave Ed fifty quid and an address and watched him walk back up the road, breaking out every now and then into a stiff little trot. Then we clambered in through Randall's window and called ahead to Si. It took us a minute to explain ourselves, we were laughing so hard.

It's strange how artists tend to have quite a clear head about hard drugs, compared to musicians, and actors – I'm sure it's all that touring and performing that does it. It sounds overly simplistic, to put it like this, but being an artist is such a solitary occupation that, when they aren't working, most artists are pretty straightforward party animals. They like to drink, they like to talk, and they like to dance. They like coke and alcohol and caffeine. The self-negation and morose quietude that goes with heroin does nothing for them. It's just not a very sociable drug, on the whole.

It is, however, seen as a dangerous drug. So, when Ed turned up at the Hackney flat of Si, aka Mr Squiffy, he was visibly shitting himself. (All this comes directly from Si, who like a lot of dealers was big into practical jokes; in other words, into power.) Si invited him in, passed him a huge spliff and sat him down on the sofa. Then he proceeded to march up and down the room, stopping to offer Ed a sample of the product, and talking up all kinds of alarming nonsense about Chinese triad gangs and batches cut with arsenic that would send you blind. Then, just after he passed the bag to Ed (a bag of flour: Si wasn't into heroin any more than we were) there was a loud banging on the door and voices yelled that it was the police. Si panicked, pulled up the sash window and shoved Ed out onto the sill, pulling the curtains closed after him.

The ensuing scene, with Si pretending to bullshit 'the police' lasted about five minutes, until they were unable to keep up the charade any longer and collapsed in fits. Poor Ed. They took a photo of him as he climbed back into the room. It's an absolute peach.

I had a copy of it with me, right there in my living room, as I sat watching Ed sit in my chair and sip my tea, nervously waiting for me to say something. I actually had my hand on the photo, in my inside jacket pocket. I had intended to bring it out and throw it down onto the coffee table, as a kind of sarcastic punch line.

That was when I thought – actually, there's nothing I could tell you about Randall that I'd trust you to tell properly. You could write a dozen

Jonathan Gibbs

books about him and not one sentence in any of them would be remotely *real*. I could do it better myself. I *should* do it.

I left the photo in my pocket and picked up my cup of tea.

'So, Ed,' I said. 'Randall. My unique perspective on my best friend Randall. My *dead* best friend Randall. What was it exactly that you wanted to know?'

Jonathan Gibbs lives in London. His writing on books has appeared in *The Independent*, *Telegraph*, *Financial Times* and *Times Literary Supplement*. He received a Malcolm Bradbury Memorial Bursary for a chapter from a now-completed novel *How Every Song Ends*. 'Ed' is not, strictly speaking, an extract from a new novel, *Randall, or The Painted Grape*.

Claire Griffiths

The Painter and the Dybbuk

Dybbuk: *In Jewish folklore, the wandering soul of a dead person that enters the body of a living person and controls his or her behaviour.*

He was as nervous as I, the night of our first sitting. He could not decide how to sit. He put his hands straight down at his sides, placed them on his knees then clasped them in his lap. He folded his arms across his chest but no, this would cover the medals that would surely come, the ones he told me I – or someone else – would add later as required. The arms returned to his side.

His face held an expression he must have thought suitably military. In truth, on one so young it looked comical. I have always subscribed to Bernini's notion that the essence of the face can be seen only when it is animated. I could not initiate a conversation – it was prohibited – yet if he did not speak there was nothing to draw. The canvas displayed but a ghost in outline: a staggered arc for the shoulders, an oval for the face, almond eyes. I clutched the pencil he had given me, poised. I waited.

I waited.

'Can I hold my gun?' Two slight vertical lines appeared between his eyebrows. I began sketching.

'If you wish.'

'You will paint it?'

'I will paint whatever you ask.'

He removed the pistol from its leather sheath, moved it from hand to hand. He placed one hand over the other and pointed it at me.

'Do you think about death *Alte Nummer*?'

'I try not to.'

'Ha, it is a good answer.' He drew the pistol towards his chest then placed it back in the holder. 'It may be too much.'

'Too much?' It was a risk to ask a direct question, but I had to keep him talking.

'Mother knows I have not used it yet. She made me promise to tell her.'

'You have not shot that gun?' The words sounded strange, an uneasy fit.

'No, they will not let me. But they will, they tell me, and soon.' He lifted his chin – his nose was exquisite. 'I am going to be a hero,' he said. 'You would do well to make it a good picture. When they let me shoot my gun I am going to be a hero and they will hang your painting in a gallery, think of that.'

I thought of that.

When the first session was finished he came to assess the results. He stood for a long time.

'My nose – it is too big,' he said. 'Make it smaller.'

'Smaller?'

'Smaller.' His voice was crisp, chilled as the winter mornings.

Though my fingers ached, *Hashem* help me, I made it smaller.

'The left ear also – it is not the same size as the right.'

The left ear was not meant to be the same size as the right, for I had angled his face to look slightly to the painting's edge. I could not draw those eyes staring straight into mine. A cool slick of sweat gathered on my brow. I enlarged the ear as requested.

'My eyes – bigger.'

The light bulb dimmed, flickered then surged back to life. The air became thick with a stench like stale breath and gone-off milk. My eyes felt the sting of the smoke from the chimneys, carried in through the open doorway.

I sketched and re-sketched, each time getting further from his true face. On and on the little corrections came – the hair, the eyelids, the lips – he convinced that at any moment the picture he wanted would appear, the one I could not see. Finally, tiredly, he seemed to admit defeat and then –

'Here! You missed a part.' Triumphantly he pointed to the base of his neck, then the picture. 'I catch out the so-called great artist, no? You miss nothing from now *Eierkopf* – understand?'

'*Eierkopf*' was a term I had heard used often. It meant 'Egghead' – intellectual – and carried the dangerous connotation of physical weakness.

'Yes, Sir.'

I inserted the missing piece: the thin strip where his white shirt collar flashed briefly above the neckline of his dull green over-jacket. I knew I had run into trouble, for white was not to be found in this place.

This was when you stirred inside me, an aching in my stomach. At first I thought it was hunger.

In the weeks that followed I assembled my palette, enlisting the help of Dietmar and Lanz, long-time prisoners, *Alte Nummer* like me. The deal was simple: the guard paid for my artistic endeavours with an extra ration of bread each day. Half of this was awarded to my helpers when a new colour was found. Whoever found white would receive the whole day's ration.

We three served in the *Sonderkommando*, responsible for pulling the new inmates from the trains. We strode through the confused crowds, confiscating suitcases, boxes and handbags, barking instructions to the crowd in Yiddish. The guards believed we were relaying their orders and so we were, but also: 'Tell the guards you are eighteen. Tell them you have a trade.'

They looked at us, bewildered, failing to understand that we were saving their lives. To those words we added: 'red/purple/blue is forbidden here. Give that to me.' Scarves, hats, gloves were handed over and pocketed, smuggled back to the barracks.

As we saw the people come into the camp, so we saw them leave. On such occasions our job was to collect the clothes before, and move the bodies after. What we could salvage we kept.

We squeezed dyes from these pilfered clothes. We crushed onion skins to powder and boiled them down in the kitchens. We strained the juice from vegetables and scraped the rust from basin pipes, ignoring the throbbing pain as nails wore down to the quick. We mixed stolen colours to pastes using oil, water – whatever we could get into our hands. But we did not, could not, find white. I crushed maggots, rocks, fingernails, but all came out yellow.

'Bones are white,' Deitmar told me once, extracting a gold tooth from a mouth, 'but only when first stripped from the skin.'

By the time of our second sitting, three brushes sat before me. One was made of straw, another feather, the final one of human hair.

I began to paint, first the backwash, an intolerable mud-brown. Occasionally a hair worked its way loose, became caught under the colour. I allowed such rogues to remain, forever trapped beneath the skin.

Hours passed; eventually I came to the collar. All I had was a fetid yellow mixture. Nevertheless, I painted.

'Can I see?'

I nodded and he approached the canvas. He halted there a long time, before his voice emerged, quiet, thin and low.

'You mean to paint me in the colours of a coward, old man?' His finger jabbed the collar. I knew it would leave a print.

'No, Sir, it is my mistake.'

'Tell me, old man, what use is a blind artist?'

I said nothing.

'I will tell you: *Hasenhupfen* – when I shoot at your feet and you dance like the hare. Then I send you to join the *Himmelfahrtskommando* – is that what you want?'

I knew what that meant, heaven-bound prisoners, those marked for execution. 'No, Sir, I do not want that.'

'Then you paint what I tell you, understand?'

'Yes, Sir.'

You stirred again inside me. A growl reverberated in my stomach. I could feel you starting to grow.

Our next sitting took place several weeks later. He strode in with purpose, soles clacking against wood.

The Painter and the Dybbuk

'I bring you a gift *Alte Nummer*.'
'Sir?'
'Boot polish – for the background.'
'Thank you, Sir.'

Slowly, I unscrewed the lid of the small round tin and gently ran a brush across the surface of the substance. It left a track like tyre marks in mud.

Thick strokes of rich dark brown swept across the canvas. Where the stitching showed, raised like Braille, it caught the light and shone, a gloss finish. Lovingly I traced the outline of his profile. The picture was beginning to take form. You danced in my belly as I painted.

During our next sitting I heard the only noise that ever came from outside the *Lager*. The same sound the rocks made as they poured from the quarry trucks; another train was coming.

I lifted my head and thought of the wagon doors opening, the stench that would hit the *Sonderkommando* on duty. My sinuses and throat felt filled with the smell, a cloud of urine, sweat and excrement. I gasped. I coughed.

'There is a problem?' he said, impatiently.
'No, Sir.'

Soon they would step down, tumbling over each other like bones. They would be pulled into groups, taken through the gates or off into the mist.

You twisted at my intestines.

I recalled my own arrival, the clothes they gave us. Dark sack cloth so loosely weaved that tiny pores of light bled through when it was held up to the sun, pin pricks in the fabric. I had never felt such roughness on my skin. The scratch which accompanied each movement told me more than anything that I was a prisoner.

You grew inside me, becoming a pressing on the bladder, an ache in my kidneys. You rose in my gut, pushed against my ribcage, wrapped your tiny fingers around my heart and squeezed.

Feed me, Zachariah, you begged. I did not know what you wanted.

That night I became a dentist, crushing grey and yellow teeth, but still no white emerged.

Claire Griffiths

Another sitting: perhaps the sixth, perhaps the seventh. How long had these meetings been taking place? I could not tell. Certainly the guard had aged. The furrow between his eyebrows remained even when his face was still. The fine creases by his eyes had multiplied, creeping beneath the sockets on thin spider legs.

As I studied this new face, you became impatient. You swelled until your breasts pushed against the inside of my torso, stretched your limbs into mine and pushed your fingers into my fingers. You stamped your little feet against the soles of my own and said feed me, Zachariah. Feed me.

'What is the matter?' His irritation startled me.

'Nothing, Sir. All is well.'

Your nails scratched at my fingertips as you pushed my hand towards the palette.

You painted over everything I had done, an exact copy, colour on colour, until it was glistening wet. Then you stopped, gently placing the brush back on the stool.

'You are finished for today?'

'No, not quite, Sir,' I heard you say, your voice now my voice.

You reached your hands towards the top of the canvas, digits touching paint.

'What are you doing?' he asked, nervously.

'Texture,' you told him.

You pulled your fingertips slowly down the painting, evenly spaced. Vertical lines raced each other down the fabric, over his face, his neck. You pressed stripes into his clothing, infesting the canvas with meaning the way that lice infested our hair. The way I had failed to do. You dipped your thumbnail in the boot polish and drew a thin stitch across his lips.

Then you retracted your limbs, crawled back inside my stomach, yawned and settled down to sleep.

'Now?'

'Yes, Sir,' I said, my voice my own once more.

He approached and stood a long time, leaning over my shoulder. Minutes passed, or perhaps just one.

'It is different,' he said eventually.

'Yes.'

Another long silence then, 'It is better, I think. It looks like a real painting.'

It was my turn to pause. 'Yes.'

'And the white?'

'The white you will have tomorrow.'

The white he would have tomorrow. The collar must be white; one tiny flash in the darkness. This was what you wanted.

Claire Griffiths graduated from UEA in 2007 with a first class degree in American Literature with Creative Writing. She works in journalism and is a features writer for the Samaritans. Her creative work has appeared in several publications including Canada's *Feathertale Review*. She is currently working on her first novel *The Gallery*.

Sue Healy

The Shit Princess

Ossie McCafferty stabbed a seagull on Trafadden Beach. The bird screamed louder than any child had ever done. His great wings pounded the ground and thrust its body at its middle-aged attacker – a movement that momentarily continued even after Ossie had sliced off its head. The fat man then dropped the knife and watched the snake of blood kiss a nearby rock pool. There was blood on his hand. Ossie made a sound that was half cry, half sigh and slipped the bloody hand down the front of his trousers.

Aoife Casey ran her palm over the shiny hide. It was almost like touching Princess Charlotte Casiraghi herself. But it was hers, Aoife Casey's own candy pink crocodile Kelly bag. She rubbed it against her cheek, breathing in the scent of varnish, of crocodiles and candy. It smelled of new.

She faced the bedroom mirror, her bag hanging on her arm like a bright pink starfish. She made a face like she was Charlotte Casiraghi setting off to town to get her Jimmy Choos fixed because she had busted a heel climbing over the Monte Carlo rocks to get out to her yacht. She swished her hair the way Charlotte Casiraghi would, because with this bag, Aoife knew she was the very spit out of Charlotte Casiraghi's own mouth.

Aoife set up her camera, put on her practised smile and posed. She held her bag in front of the two little lumps of fat that recently stretched her T-shirt. They would have to go into a bra soon. But that would mean going into a shop to ask for one. Maybe she could ask Mounty Carlow to send her a designer bra instead. There was a dull thud as a seagull dropped shit on the window. The bird glided down to the beach.

Whenever the tide was out, Aoife would take the short-cut home from school across the beach. She would sit by the rock pools and blow air across their surface, watching the water wrinkle. Fringes of mussels guarded the rims of the pools like gapped-toothed battlements on a fabulous castle. Within, there were wonderlands of purple sea flowers and feathers of lime green growth. Knobs of ruby sea squirts sucked blood from the rocks, wee starfish sprinkled the sandy beds like chips of jewels and pink baby crabs flew through mountains of limpets. Aoife would fish out these little creatures and let them tickle her cold fingers as they ran around her hand looking for the sea. She would put them back for the turning of the tide, when the water would crash down on the pools one by one, scooping up their contents. Aoife imagined the starfish and crabs swimming away into the ocean like a shoal of Smarties.

The mussels never left, however. Those dull shells clung to the rocks and survived on shit. They said the biggest mussels were up the estuary where the city sewerage slushed into the mouth of the sea. You got mussels the length of your hand there.

If the tide was in, however, Aoife had to go past the barrel shed. The girls would be there smoking, talking and copying homework. And, like a starting gun at a race, a comment from Clodagh Slattery would set them all off.

'Well Aoife. How's shit?'
'Smell of shit around here, lads.'
'Shit happens, Aoify.'
'Sure as shit does.'
They all knew.

On the night it happened, her father was in a bad state by early evening. He sat behind the bar with his head on the counter. Daithi Gallagher and Tommy Cullen were soon helping themselves to drinks, as were a carload of Dubliners who thought it was all very funny and that

Sue Healy

it was always funny like that down the country.

'Iffta goo,' said her father.

'What's that you're saying, boy?' said Daithi. 'Lads, I think our landlord is going to sing us a song. Go on Pat, give us an aul' bar.'

'Ffta,' he said.

Daithi and Tommy kept on talking. He walked out from behind the bar, pulling his trousers down as he did. Then it sploshed out of him, like silage spurting out a shoot.

'For fuck sake, Pat. Ah, Jesus. Ach, Pat, that is fucking disgusting. For fuck sake,' they chorused.

'Jaysus,' said the carload from Dublin.

Daithi and Tommy grabbed an arm each and threw him out the door of his own pub.

'Jesus wept. Aoife, there is some mess out here, girl,' Daithi shouted into Aoife in the back room.

They did not have to tell her, she had seen it all from the backroom. Aoife came out with her hot face and mopped the floor. The carload's eyes rolled all over her. She followed the brown trail streeling out the door. Her father lay on the steps like storm kelp. His arms were twisted around his back, his trousers around his knees and his mouth knitted to the step by threads of drool. His arse was still dripping. She took her coat from inside the doorway and threw it over him.

The carload stepped over him as they rushed away to Dublin, laughing like seagulls as they went for their car. She watched them speed so fast down the hill they nearly went into Peadar Kearney's tree.

After a while, Daithi put him on the parlour floor and shoved a doormat under his head. Aoife went to her bedroom. She listened to the sea pushing away from Trafadden and she heard the seagulls at dawn. They laughed about the shitting and screamed it all around the village. She heard his bedroom door shut mid-morning. He did not come out for a day. The pub went the following month.

Aoife went online now. She uploaded her new photograph with the bag. Then she googled for images of "Charlotte Casiraghi".

Mounty Carlow popped up on a chat window.

'Hello Princess Aoife. Did the handbag arrive?'

The Shit Princess

'Dis morning post. OMG. Tnx Mounty Carlow!!!!'
'Grand. So, I got the address right?'
'Its de bizniz.'
'Can u send me through a photo, Princess?'
Aoife sent on the image.
'U r a very beautiful girl, Princess. But do you have one of u in the blue dress you were wearing in that first photo you sent me?'
'No, wearin jeans 2day.'
'Can u put on the blue dress for me?'
'That's an old blu dress from when I was 10 + a half and it prob wont fit + I horrible in it.'
'Impossible, nothing cd b horrible on u, Princess. '

Aoife tried to put on the dress, but the swelling of her baby breasts meant she could not zip it up at the back. Maybe Mounty Carlow would buy her a new dress once he saw it. She sent the image through.

Quite a while passed, Aoife had started her homework by the time Mounty Carlow returned.

'Hey, Princess. I am in love with u!'
'LOL.'
'Really, Princess, I think it is time we met.'
'LOL.'
'What's so funny?'
 'U live in Monaco. How 2 meet?'
'I have a house in Ireland too. I can fly over in my private jet.'
'Yeah? Where is your house?'
'Next door to Bono in Dublin.'
'OMG, Bono?'
'Sure. Would u like to meet him?'
'OK.'
'Tomorrow?'
'OK.'
'I can pick u up in my private van.'
'Here? In Trafadden?'
'Sure. Tomorrow morning at 09:00?'
'Tmrw's Satrdy. Cn we meet at 11?'
'That's OK, Princess. Can you meet me by the old telephone box after

Sue Healy

the bus stop by the crossroads?'

'Sure! Can't wait Mounty Carlow!'

Mounty Carlow did not answer. Aoife changed back in to her jeans. Downstairs she heard a door opening. Her father was home.

She went down. He was sitting at the kitchen table looking out at the sky, like it was interesting.

'Hi.'

He jumped and turned to her. He was pale.

'Hey, little Aoify, sorry I didn't hear you come down, love.'

He looked at her for longer than normal. She frowned and moved towards the cupboard.

'How are you, Aoify?'

She opened a tin of beans.

'Grand, why?'

'I'm, well, just want to know.'

'Yeah. Is beans-on-toast all right for you?'

'Yes, lovely. I'm not that hungry though, love. I might just have a cup of tea.'

'Suit yourself.'

His head trembled. He kept his eyes on her. She turned to put the bread in the toaster. He spoke to her back.

'Aoife, I, I've been meaning to tell you, I haven't had a drink since Monday. I just want you to know that, pet.'

Her stomach tightened like pulled shoelaces.

'Whatever,' she said.

'Well, I, I'm meeting up with some people tonight who, well, who don't drink.'

'OK.'

'I won't be long, pet.'

'OK.'

'Maybe we'll do something together tomorrow? We could walk over to the headland, would you like that, Princess? It's, well, it's been hard since your mother left, Pet, but it is going to change now.'

She shrugged her shoulders.

Aoife took her beans-on-toast back to her room. She lifted up the candy pink crocodile Kelly bag, opened all the zips, pulled out the tissue stuffing and read every detail on the label inside. She wondered if Taiwan was in Monaco and if the designer who made the bag was a model with a yacht. She put the bag on the dresser where she could see it from her pillow. She kicked her mussel-coloured schoolbag under the bed.

Ossie felt calm when he woke in his camper van that morning. So still, he thought he would be able to drive back to Cork with nothing more from his trip to Trafadden than the seagull's head that lay on top of his laptop. He thought it might really be different this time. But as the sun rolled up the sky, the tickling in his thighs started. He considered trying to quell it again with another seagull but there were none in sight. The feeling spun into his stomach. It rushed to his face and ran around his head, knocking on his forehead. It jingled like bells in his fingers. And it raged in his groin. His eyes filled. It was too late.

He sniffled, started the camper van's engine. His vision was blurred, his cheeks damp. He eased out of the car park and rolled the van down to the crossroads. The vehicle jerked in and out of a pothole and his head hit the roof. His eyes dried. His knuckles went white and his foot nudged the accelerator.

The seagull appeared at his windscreen as sudden as a ghost. Ossie swerved to the left and the last sight he ever saw was Peadar Kearney's tree. The last sound he heard was the screech of seagull laughter.

Ten whole songs had played on Aoife's iPod while she waited by the crossroads. The rain spat down. Her top was nearly see-through now. She hugged her candy pink crocodile Kelly bag to her chest. She could feel the mascara, that she was not allowed to wear, dribbling down her cheeks and she was thinking about what Bono was going to say when he saw the state of her, when a seagull dropped a great dollop of green and white shit on her candy pink crocodile Kelly bag. That did it, the tears and snot came dribbling and the sobs put-putted out of her. A car pulled up.

'Well Aoife,' said Clodagh Slattery.
'Well Clodagh,' sobbed Aoife.
'Get in the back, love,' said Clodagh Slattery's mother.
'Looks like the shit's goin' down,' said Clodagh, nodding at her shit-

covered bag.

'Clodagh!' said her mother, 'Aoife Casey, there's a day to be walking around without a coat. Are you on your way home from the Waterford bus?'

'Yeah,' sniffled Aoife.

'We can drop you up home,' said the mother. 'You're in luck. We only came this way because there has been some kind of accident on Ballyhale Hill. How's your Dad doing?'

'Shit,' said Clodagh.

'Clodagh!' said the Mother.

'Shit,' sobbed Aoife.

Sue Healy, b. 1970, is Irish. She spent a decade in Budapest working as a journalist and has also worked in Paris. Her short story *I Am Not A Muse* was published in the *New European Writing* anthology. Sue recently completed a stageplay and is working on her novel *Trafadden*.

Stephen Hepplestone

The Russian Game
An excerpt from a novel

The Russian game is a work-in-progress novel set in contemporary England. It is about the coming of age of Robin Smith, a young man addicted to taking excessive risks, addicted to playing 'Russian games'. In this excerpt it is 1990, Rob is nine years old and he is playing with his action figures.

It is Sunday afternoon and it is sunny and so all the children should be playing out but they can't because the village is full of baddies, so everybody is scared.

Skeletor is banging on the bakery window.

'Let me in,' he says. 'I want some bread.'

He really is very hungry. He hasn't eaten for a long time, but the people in the bakery won't let him in because they are frightened.

The Joker is locked in the Sheriff's office because the Joker has been bad. Darth Vader is going to let the Joker out because Darth Vader is bored. If Darth Vader and the Joker team up then they will do all sorts of bad things. They will call people names, and hit people, and swear, and steal cars and things. Somebody needs to stop Darth Vader!

But then Batman comes along. Batman is in a bad mood and he is very big, much bigger than the people who live in the village, and bigger than Darth Vader and the Joker and Skeletor.

'I'm Batman,' he says, 'I don't like your village because it's too small and I can't fit into anything.'

He tries to open the door to the post office but his hand is too big, and he tries to climb into the barn, but he just does not fit in. He is in such a bad mood that he starts to jump up and down on the village. His big feet bang into Skeletor and Darth Vader and they shout at him and call him names but he is making lots of noise so he cannot hear them.

'I'm Batman,' he says, 'and I don't like this village and so I'm going to break it.'

He keeps on jumping on the houses and the buildings. Bash! Smash! Crash! Batman breaks the Sheriff's office and the Joker jumps out.

'Hello Batman,' he says. 'Why did the chicken cross the road?'

'I don't know, Joker. Why did the chicken cross the road?'

'Because it was nailed to the Batman's foot,' the Joker says and, pow! He kicks Batman's big toe and Batman jumps up in the air and because his toe hurts so much he starts to cry, and because he is crying he runs away.

Darth Vader is laughing a lot at what the Joker did to the Batman.

'You really think I'm funny, don't you Darth Vader?' the Joker says.

'Oh yes. You're the funniest baddie ever,' says Darth Vader.

'Thank you. Here have some chewing gum.'

But it is trick chewing gum and when Darth Vader touches it he gets an electric shock. ZZZ!

Then Batman comes back and he is even more angry than he was before.

'I'm going to get you Joker,' he says and tries to jump on the Joker but the Joker runs away and Batman squishes Darth Vader by accident.

Batman tries to jump on the Joker again but the Joker moves and Batman hits the bakery and the door opens and so Skeletor goes inside and eats all of the bread.

The Baker is scared but he says, 'That's one pound and fifty pence you owe me.'

'But I only get fifty pence a week pocket money!' Skeletor says and then runs away really fast.

Batman is still trying to jump on the Joker, but the Joker keeps moving and Batman keeps breaking things. Crash! Bash! Smash! The whole village will be broken soon unless someone stops him.

Then, hurray! The goodies come to save the day. She-Ra and He-Man are sat on top of Battle Cat and Battle Cat roars as loud as he can, and Darth Vader and Batman and the Joker and Skeletor all turn to look at He-

Man and She-Ra.

'Stop fighting everyone,' says She-Ra.

'Do as you're told,' says He-Man. 'And listen to what She-Ra tells you. Stop fighting or else.'

'Or else what?' says the Joker.

'We'll ground you, and we'll stop your pocket money and we'll tell you off,' says He-Man.

'He started it,' Batman says. 'He kicked my toe.'

'Never mind who started it,' says She-Ra. 'You should all know better, especially you Batman, you're supposed to be a goodie.'

'I'm sorry,' says Batman.

'What about you?' She-Ra says to the Joker. 'Are you going to apologise to Batman?'

'I'm really very sorry,' says the Joker to Batman. 'Let's shake hands and be friends.'

But the Joker is holding an electric buzzer, and so when Batman shakes the Joker's hand he gets an electric shock, ZZZZZZZZ!

Then everyone starts fighting. Batman starts trying to squash the Joker again and He-Man gets into a fight with Darth Vader and Skeletor. Bash! Smash! Crash!

She-Ra tries to stop Batman from squashing the Joker, but she can't stop him because he is so big and she really needs He-Man to help but he is still fighting Darth Vader and Skeletor, and so it looks like the village is going to get really broken.

But then another goodie comes to save the day and this time it is the best goodie, it is Optimus Prime! He is the best because he is a big, red and blue robot and can transform into a lorry. He can transform into a lorry because he is a Transformer. He can also transform into a base so that he can fix things and robots and people and make them better.

'I am Optimus Prime,' he says. 'I'm the king of the special robot space police. Everybody stop fighting and look at this,' he says in his deep, robot voice.

Everybody does as they are told because of Optimus Prime's big voice, even the Joker.

Everybody is looking at him so Optimus Prime transforms into a lorry, then into the base, then into the Lorry again, then he transforms back

Stephen Hepplestone

into a robot.

'Batman,' Optimus says and transforms into the base, 'I know you are angry because you do not fit in anywhere in the village but if you behave yourself and act like a goodie again then I will help you build a secret bat-car to drive in and a bat-cave to live in.'

And to show Batman that he really could help, Optimus uses his special fixing tools to fix the bakery door.

'Thank you Optimus Prime, I promise I'll behave myself and act like a goodie again,' Batman says.

Optimus Prime transforms back into a Robot and then speaks to Darth Vader, Skeletor and the Joker.

'If you lot don't stop being so naughty then I'll blast you with my laser gun. I don't want to, but I will if you carry on, just you wait and see,' he says.

Because he has such a big, deep voice and because he can transform and because he is a robot, and because he shoots them with his laser for a bit, all the baddies do as they are told.

'You've got to learn how to express your anger in other ways,' Optimus Prime says to Batman and Skeletor. 'You can't go getting into fights all the time and you can't go around taking whatever you want, no matter how hungry you are. You'll end up in prison, like the Joker.'

Skeletor gets a job at the bakery to pay back the money he owes. Darth Vader and the Joker tell jokes to make everyone laugh – nice jokes, not mean ones – and soon the village is fixed. Then Optimus Prime transforms into a base and fixes everyone, makes them all better.

Once She-Ra has been fixed she jumps off Optimus Prime and shouts 'Kiss Chase' and all the boys run away because they hate kissing. But She-Ra catches He-Man and pins him to the ground and kisses him all over his face.

'Urgh,' says He-Man, 'Get off me She-Ra, I don't even like girls.'

But She-Ra won't get off and she keeps kissing He-Man and the Joker laughs at them.

'She-Ra and He-Man up a tree, K-I-S-S-I-N-G,' he sings and everybody laughs.

Then, because they have kissed, She-Ra and He-Man get married and because they are married, they have babies. The children are smaller than He-Man and She-Ra, apart from the littlest child, he looks a lot like He-Man, but he is different. He is Battle Damage He-Man. He has a special part in his chest that spins around when he is hit and shows cracks and battle damage.

At first He-Man and She-Ra take care of the children but then, even though they are goodies, He-Man and She-Ra start fighting all the time. She-Ra runs away and the children think they will never see their mummy again and so they are very upset and start to cry and run around and look for her, but then She-Ra comes back.

'You lot didn't half make a racket. I could hear you from the graveyard. I only went for a walk,' she says.

The children are happy but then She-Ra and He-Man start fighting again and He-Man starts to fight the children, but because the children are small, He-Man beats them very easily and even though She-Ra tries to stop him, and even though She-Ra is beautiful and magical, she is not as big or as strong or as angry as He-Man, and so She-Ra and the children get hurt all the time, and the littlest child, Battle Damage He-Man, his chest bit spins to show the battle damage, and so all the people in the village can see that he is hurt, but they don't do anything to help.

Then She-Ra runs away again and even though the children run around the garden crying and calling out for their mummy, she does not come back straight away. She does not come back for a long time and the children are very sad and scared and hungry. The children have to make their own dinner and wash their own clothes, and they have to do everything very quietly because He-Man is still very angry, and the biggest sister gets very tired because she has to do all of the things that a mummy does but she is only a sister.

Optimus Prime does not notice anything because he is too busy helping Batman build his cave and so, the littlest child, Battle Damage He-Man, decides to sneak out to ask Optimus Prime if he can fix him, if he can make him better so that he can make He-Man and She-Ra be friends again.

But then She-Ra comes back and she has brought someone with her, she has brought Superman.

Stephen Hepplestone is from the North of England. He is twenty-eight years old. After completing the MA he intends to continue writing his first novel.

UEA Creative Writing Anthology 2009

Philip Langeskov

The Man Who Lives in the Woods

TOMORROW, YOU WILL leave work on time. In the car park you will stand for a few moments, the heels of your shoes sinking into the soft tarmac, and you will wonder if this oppressive heat can possibly continue. After stopping to buy a packet of razor blades, you will take the long road home, the one that runs between the edge of town and the river bank. On a bench opposite the swings, you will see a young girl – about nine, auburn hair, summer dress – balancing precariously on one leg. With half an ear you will listen to the evening news. The hottest July on record. Days of soaring heat. Beaches – at Scarborough, at Whitstable, at Lowestoft – packed long into the evenings. Unusual readying patterns are evident in migrant birds.

After parking the car in the garage, you will walk up the path to be greeted by the looming faces of your children. As you enter they will run and jump in circles around your feet, babbling at you like a pair of restive dogs. The back door will slam shut behind you.

At the kitchen counter your husband will be preparing supper, a knife in his hand and a partially chopped onion on the board in front of him.

'I need another thirty minutes if you want to change,' he will say.

'Do I get a kiss?'

He will approach you, the knife still in his hand, and hold you in his arms. The children will flock around you, moving in and out, trying to wriggle their frames into the space between your bodies.

'Lila's got a surprise for you.'

'Really?'

'Look.'

You will turn to your daughter as she moves across the kitchen. She is holding something behind her back.

'Not now, darling,' you will say. 'Mummy's got to change.'

Upstairs in the bedroom, you will lean against the wall as you slip off your shoes. You will step out of your skirt and, folding it once, throw it on the bed. You will take a pair of jeans from the chest of drawers under the mirror, the ones that stop halfway down your calves. The denim will feel cool against your skin and the stitching of the pockets will snag against your underwear. From the pile in the wardrobe you will choose a vest top. You will go to the window. Leaning out, you will let down your hair and listen to the warm buzz of evening. On your way back down you will almost step on the cat, who is sleeping against the bottom stair in a shaft of sunlight.

The kitchen will be full of the aroma of frying onions and spices.

'What are we having?'

'That chicken curry. The one with the fried onion sauce.'

'Curry? In this weather? I thought we'd have a salad.'

He will stand back, your husband, with his arms folded and give you that look he gives you.

'Right,' you will say. 'Are we having wine?'

Outside in the garden, the surface of the pond ripples as the shadow of a fish moves through the water

'You can. I'm having beer. There's white in the fridge.'

'Mummy,' your son will call.

'Yes, Joe. What is it?'

'Mummy. Cat's dead.'

'No, he isn't. He's just sleeping.'

'He's dead.'

You and your husband will laugh as you put the cork back in the wine bottle. With the glass in your hand you will go through to the hall. Joseph will be standing, wearing his serious face.

'He's just sleeping, Joe. See. His tummy's going up and down.'

Joseph will get down on his knees and crawl into the sunlight, before curling up in a ball beside the cat. You will crouch down alongside him.

Minutes will pass.

You will not see Lila standing behind you, watching as you stroke the sleeve of Joseph's shirt.

'It's ready.'
'Coming. Lila, Joe. Come on. Dinner time.'
Over supper, Lila will give you a piece of purple paper with two furious, waxy, yellow scrawls on it, one larger than the other.
'What's this?' you will say, pointing to the smaller scrawl.
'Mummy.'
'And what's this one?'
'Daddy.'
'Mummy and Daddy. Isn't that nice.'
After supper, you will bathe the children while your husband washes up. Lila will be fine while she's in the bath. It will only be afterwards, when you are trying to get her into bed, that she begins to play up. She will stand in the middle of the room and turn her face to the wall. She will absolutely refuse to have her teeth brushed, clamping her mouth tightly shut. When you do get her into bed, she will not accept a story, not from you.

Across the landing, Joseph will be waiting.
'I'm hot.'
'I know, Joe. But the window's open. There's a bit of a breeze.'
'I won't be able to sleep.'
'Why don't you have a sheet instead of the duvet?'
'I like the duvet.'
'That's why you're hot, though.' You will put your hand on his forehead, brushing the hair from his eyes. 'You are warm.' You will turn your hand over, brushing the cool of your knuckles against his clammy skin.
'Sleeptime. Lights out.'
When you get downstairs, your husband will be finishing up, his meticulous hands wiping the surfaces with a sponge. The dinner plates and dessert bowls will be stacked neatly on the side above the cupboard.
'Your princess wants a story. And Joe's all feverish. That curry was too much for him.'
'Don't be ridiculous.'

While your husband tells your daughter a story, you will sit in the lounge. The shadows on the lawn creep towards the window. On the table, a leaflet about the carnival weekend. There will be a parade of floats on Saturday, and a festival of flowers at the town hall.

By the time your husband comes down it will nearly be half past eight.

'She all right?'

'She's fine. You just need to be patient with her.'

In the silence that follows, while your husband flicks through the television guide, you will read about the fair, this coming Sunday, on the open ground by the quay. Last year, Joseph came home with two goldfish in a bag.

'There's that thing at nine.'

'What thing?'

'About icebergs. Remember?'

Suddenly   you won't even know you are – you will stand.

'I'm going for a drive.'

'You're what?'

'I'm going for a drive.'

You will walk quickly through the kitchen. The back door will stick and you will have to force it open. Outside, the heat will still be heavy in the air.

You will drive towards town. When you reach the market square, you will take the left turn that leads towards the hospital. At the traffic lights you will turn right, taking the back road out to the country. You will pass the kennels and the Fox Inn. Its hanging baskets will sway at the roadside as you speed past. Soon, Reetham Church will be ahead of you, its fine flint bell tower standing square against the streaky evening sky. The road bends sharply at the bottom of Shadingfield Hill. With your window wound all the way down you will breathe in the scent – a dusty sweetness – that rises from the wheat fields. Even with the window open you will feel the heat, the force of it, as it rushes into the car.

As you pass what used to be the Munday farm, you will remember the time you went there as a child. It was Christmas; there was a turkey to be bought. Your father prowled the rear courtyard, his boots up to his knees. You followed him and the flock of birds that gathered reached almost to your waist.

'Pick one, my princess,' your father said.

After a mile, you will begin to slow down. You are looking out for the white concrete post, the one that marks the route of the old London mainline. Beyond it, on the left, you will see the opening of the road to the woods. It runs down a shallow incline to a ford that crosses a stream and then dips under a canopy of trees. Flashes of sunlight will cast spots of white across the dashboard. In open ground again, with fields of yellow rape on both sides, you will lower the visor to counter the sun. When you reach the turning point – a semi-circle of gravel on the left-hand side of the road – you will pull in.

You will walk to the gap in the hedge and follow the path that leads back up to the woods. The mud beneath your feet will be cracked and parched, almost sandy in places. The light will begin to fade. You will notice the chill as you enter the wood. The trees are densely packed, the ground in permanent shadow. At the brow of the hill, the trees give way, opening out like a curtain to reveal the landscape ahead. You will sit on a grey carpet of dirt. Broken twigs and fragments of pine cone will prick your palms as you settle into place. The earth will feel cool through the seat of your jeans. You will light a cigarette, your last. Your husband would kill you if he knew. Away to the west, the sun will be setting. You will draw your knees up to your chest and look out over the fields and the hedgerows. You will sense the atmosphere, a crackling in the air, the click of insect wings.

Years ago, walking ... with your father, you stopped at this very spot. You were nine. It was autumn, nearly winter. A bank of leaves shivered against the upturned stump of a tree. Crouching low, with one arm around your shoulder, your father pointed to the fields below, his thick muddy fingers quivering in the air.

There's the tower of Witchingham Church. That field over there used to belong to your grandfather. In the corner of that field, near the water butt, an armed robber was caught by a policeman on a commandeered bike. It made the national news. And there. Over there. In that clump of trees by the irrigation pond. Can you see? He's in there.

Who's in there?

A man.

What man?
An old man.
Who is he?
It's a secret.
Tell me.
Only if you promise not to tell a single soul.
I promise.
Well. They say he's been alive since the beginning of time. That he has a beard that reaches down to his knees. He can only be seen at twilight, his figure flickering in the shadows as he skips across the fields. His house is made from jam jars and twisted pieces of metal. He keeps a fire going day and night – look! there! you can see the smoke.
What does he do?
He does his work.
What's his work?
He weaves wishes. That's what they say. He just sits there, weaving wishes. When he has enough, he gathers them up and puts them in an old leather satchel that hangs from a branch of a tree. Then – every night, at just this time – he sneaks out, his satchel slung across his shoulder.
What happens to the wishes?
I'm coming to that. They say that he is able to leap across the sky, as if carried on a shooting star. As he leaps, he lets the wishes cascade from his bag and they fall to the ground like snow.
That's silly.
It's not silly. It's absolutely true. If you look very carefully you might be able to see him. They say that if you see a wish, you get to keep it for yourself. You can keep it forever if you like, but you can only use it once – just once.
But what's his name?
His name? He doesn't have a name. He's the man who lives in the woods.

Philip Langeskov was born in Copenhagen in 1976 and grew up on the Norfolk/Suffolk border. His writing has appeared in *The Decadent Handbook* (Dedalus, 2006) and *Bad Idea Magazine*. 'The Man Who Lives in the Woods' is from the collection, *Tonight, Sometime*. He received the 2008 David Higham Award.

Alex Lewis

In California, 1966

It was a day bleached by summer heat. Isaac knuckled the sweat from where it pooled at his brow. He was slender, sandy-haired, tan: dirt is mounded around him and he sat with his knees drawn to his chest, absorbing the placid drawl of a Lon Simmons baseball game. 'We've been in a rain delay for three hours now,' the announcer says. 'Of course, Queen Victoria reigned for sixty years. So what do we have to complain about?' Isaac laughed as he thumbed through his cards. Willie Mays, Willie McCovey, Orlando Cepeda, Juan Marichal, Jim Ray Hart; each image grinned or glared. A cicada called, drowning out Simmons and the softer sounds of a dry breeze caught in the evergreens.

The radio's chrome surface was dull and dusty. Adjusting its antennae scalded his fingers. Isaac twisted the volume dial and Simmons's voice crackled out in a baritone. Listening took place in the middle of the slope that rolled up from Isaac's house and into the surrounding hills. As the game continued, Isaac dealt out the corresponding characters, every batter and every pitcher. The sun set slowly – over its course, Isaac's shirt soaked through with sweat. His body cooled as twilight finally settled in and Simmons signed off on the broadcast. A truck rumbled up the driveway. Isaac collected his things, turned off the radio, and raced inside.

The way back into Isaac's home led through a white and winding corridor that opened into a dirty tile kitchen. Abe Logan, Isaac's stepfather, rustled through the new refrigerator. 'You take that radio out there again?' Abe chewed though a bare slice of deli meat. He gestured Isaac toward the counter. 'Christ's sake, put it up. Your mother buys something nice and you go get crud all over it.' Abe wore cowboy boots, faded jeans and a plaid work shirt tucked into his belt. Coming close to his stepfather caused Isaac's nose to wrinkle. It was the smell of whiskey that churned Isaac's stomach. The sickly sweetness of it was heavy on Abe's breath. 'Come along, son. Your mother and sister are at the lake.'

The two made their wordless way through the plain, beige living room and out the front door. Isaac kept his cards, stuffing the deck into his back left pocket. The single lane road which wound from their house disappeared into the density of the woodlands. Abe's truck was rugged and red, unadorned save for some mud stains around the wheel wells, a few dents, and a single bumper sticker bearing white-on-black print: 'There Ain't No Home But My Own.' Insects veered about in the porch lamp light, a few June Beetles taking a rude beeline for Isaac's chest and forehead. He was relieved by entering the cab and shutting the door, though the smell of whiskey was strong in there, leavened by cigarette butts and empty cans of chewing tobacco. Abe turned the ignition and gravel crackled as the vehicle accelerated, pulling into the wilderness.

For a minute or two, Abe drove without his lights, and Isaac watched the dark forms of trees whistle by on either side. Igniting the beams illuminated the green and brown borders, but made the surroundings into a tunnel of motion. Abe drove with his knees and used his hands to roll down the window and take a finger's worth of chew from the tin he kept in his breast pocket. Isaac thought about Willie Mays catching line drives and Jim Ray Hart hitting homeruns into the stiff Pacific wind.

The deer seemed to drop straight from the sky, landing on the bumper with the base of its neck; its body bent away and around the nose of the truck. 'Ah, damn!' Abe shouted before slowing into a rocky turnout. Soil for the pull-off and pieces of the dying doe surrounded the truck, though mostly it all looked like night. Abe pointed at the glove compartment. 'Get that for me,' he said. Inside was a Colt revolver, silver steel with a grip of unpolished wood, and two maps of the Sierra Nevada. Isaac took the pistol and handed it to Abe, who used it to motion Isaac outside. 'Come on,' he said. Motes floated around them and the bugs descended, including some red-eyed flies that began to crawl along the twitching body. Standing there, they saw the injury all over the animal's spine. Abe frowned and offered his handgun to Isaac. 'Go ahead,' Abe said. Aiming the weapon required several tries. Isaac drew the hammer of the thing close to his collarbone, held it there and quavered in the space ahead of pushing the barrel toward the creature's sagging chest. 'Put him out of his misery,' Abe said.

Isaac could not see the deer's face. Its whole back was basked in highlight, legs swimming mechanically in the air, its muscles bunching and uncurling beneath torn tufts of fur. He leveled the gun sights at its shoulders, but his fingers stammered around the hold and trigger for two minutes before Abe relieved him and, with a sigh, blew out the animal's brain. Abe hefted the carcass by the torso. Isaac stood by, eyes tracking the point where the creature had been shot and the stain it made as its wound pressed against his stepfather's sleeve. Isaac stepped forward and reached for the loosely dangling hooves, but froze and wound up with his hands in his pockets. Abe finished loading the body and hopped back into the driver's seat.

Driving slung the corpse back and forth in a racket across the plane of the bed. After a few minutes the lake appeared: the lights of rental residences in the distance, the smell of French fries and hamburgers radiating from the low build of the Forks Restaurant. Abe pulled into the elevated lip bathed by the Forks' glare of advertisement and early dinner bustle, exited and began to shout for a butcher. There were cabins and camping all about the near part of the lake, as well as a pier for fishermen and pleasure boaters, draped in blue evening. Isaac slipped out and across the driving lane situated between the dock and the resort, crossed down the wooden steps which ran over the beach and then along the pontoon and redwood boards that led two hundred feet into the water. A few vacationers were slumped near their vessels, drinking beer. Isaac walked past them, to the gas pump which sat at the launch station. Reeds poked out from all around the jetty. Fish splashed and crowds of duck and geese massed along the sand behind him, squawking in chorus with the other birds who roosted in the trees that surrounded the dip of the Bass Lake reservoir.

It was out there that his mother found him. She stood at his back and ran her fingers through his hair. 'I heard you did a big thing today,' she said. 'Thank you so much, sweetie.'

Alex Lewis took his undergraduate degree in Creative Writing at the University of California, Riverside. He is a published freelance journalist and is working on his first novel. Alex currently lives in Budapest, Hungary.

In California, 1966

Seònaid MacKay

Nightfeeder
Extract from a short story

It's dark again. I must have fallen asleep on the chair. The hissing on the monitor seems to have become louder and it fills my head. There's no noise from the baby but I get a feeling, as if I should go and check on him.

I go upstairs to his bedroom. The bedside table and the Moses basket are lit by the orange glow of the monitor and I can see that he is wide awake, lying there silently, his eyes black and glittering. He seems to be looking directly at me. It's almost as if he's going to speak and say something like, oh hello.

The room is stale – sort of an animal smell – and it's very warm. I'll have to remember to give it an airing tomorrow, to open the windows.

I pick him up and unwrap his swaddling. He clings to me with his thin little arms and legs. I undo my nightdress and put him to my breast. The pain in my breast gradually subsides as he drains me and I feed him for what must be over an hour. When he's finished, I move him to the other breast and he drains that too.

He's still sucking and I know there's no more milk, so I cuddle him and then go to put him back in the basket, but he keeps clinging to me. I try to pull him off, but he won't budge. I pull harder, and still he grips, his arms and legs digging into my torso. I pull again, and this time I give him a little jerk as I do so. This dislodges him and I quickly put him in the basket. He wriggles and squirms and I can feel the muscles moving under his skin as I fold the sheet around his body, trying to pin his arms down by his sides. Because he's struggling, it's difficult to do this properly and before I know it, one arm has thrust upwards from the swaddling, the fingers outstretched and feeling in the air towards me. I push the arm back down by his body and hold it there hard as I wrap the sheet, more firmly this time. He doesn't make any noise while I do this and once he's tightly swaddled, he shuts his eyes. I go through to the other room and get into bed. I've taken the receiver with me and I place it on my bedside table.

The baby monitor amplifies and compresses any noise that it picks up. A car passes by the front drive and it sounds like a prowling animal. The sheep in the fields sound too close, as if a flock of them are gathered underneath the baby's window, looking up.

I lie on the sheets, unable to sleep, listening to the monitor. It constantly hisses now that everything is silent, as if thousands of sound particles are moving restlessly against each other, waiting for the chance to configure into some other, more solid noise.

I'm wide awake now and it feels like I'm all alone with myself. I'm not sure what time it is, but I guess it must be around two o'clock in the morning. It's hot, even for a summer's night.

I go downstairs to the kitchen to get a drink. I search on the wall for the light switch, then go over to the sink. The room is too bright and I squint until my eyes stop watering. I turn on the tap and let the water run cold, then I place a tumbler under the flow. I misjudge the force of the water and it shoots out of the glass and up my arm, soaking my nightdress. I catch sight of my reflection in the window. The light is right over my head, my eyes are lost in black sockets and my skin looks very white. My nightdress hangs, shapeless and stained.

I go to the wall and switch off the light.

I stand there until my eyes become accustomed to the gloom. I walk back up to the sink. The window is no longer a dark mirror and now I can see through it to the moonlit landscape beyond.

The fields are soft grey shapes, and suspended above them is a smudge of moon. The trees are black silhouettes against the sky. The reservoir gleams like mirrored glass.

Maybe I could open the window, climb out and disappear.

I reach for the handle.

There's a movement close to my body, as if there's something shifting around in the darkness.

I hold my breath. Everything slows as the darkness solidifies around me.

There is something in here, watching me.

I stand very still.

Something is pacing around the edges of the room, like an animal.

My pulse is throbbing in my wrists.

I force myself to move.

I run out of the kitchen.

I run up the stairs.

I get back into bed.

I shouldn't be so stupid. There's nothing to be scared of. It's just because I'm tired.

I think I was nearly about to drift off, when something makes me come to. I've got that feeling again, so I go and check on him. He's doing the same thing as before: lying there, awake, his mouth making that sucking motion, his eyes wide and moving around. And just like last time, he hasn't made a sound.

I pick him up again and feed him, for longer this time. I rest against the pillows as I nurse him, watching the gap in the curtains turn from black to purple to pink.

It's early morning and already it is bright. I must have dropped off to sleep. A slice of yellow light burns between the curtains. The baby is still lying against my breast, sleeping. His mouth is wide open and resting on my nipple: both are coated with sticky, congealed milk. I sit up with a start.

I put him back in his basket then I go downstairs and make myself a coffee. The light is streaming in through the kitchen window, illuminating the edges of everything with a pale, lemony gold. I look out at the back garden and the old wall – all that remains of the old estate that these houses were built on – and then the view of the whole valley.

There are a few other houses dotted on the outer edges of the

Seònaid MacKay

development, anonymous white boxes, just like this one. Beyond that there is the moorland. I follow the line of the burn that cuts through the fields, running down to the reservoir at the bottom of the valley, and then I look up at the pale hills in the distance.

Apart from the few houses, the sheep and the reservoir, there's very little else in the way of civilization that I can see from this window. It makes it easy to imagine this place when there was no human trace on the land, nothing except for bog, reeds and mist.

Before the baby was born, when I'd just bought this place, I used to climb over the back garden wall and go exploring in the moors on my own. It's a harsh landscape. I liked to go walking until I got a strange feeling that I'd gone too far: then I'd turn and head home. When I got back indoors, I'd find myself appreciating the things that can normally make me feel claustrophobic: central heating, carpet, the general household hum of lights and plug sockets. This feeling never lasted though, and I'd soon find myself out walking again.

The sun is bright outside. I wash the baby's bedding, trying to get rid of that smell. He's upstairs and he cries the whole time, but when I go upstairs to feed him, he refuses to latch on to my breast, and just cries more loudly. I come back downstairs and look at an old magazine, read an article, but he's still crying and I can't concentrate. I can't have slept for longer than two hours at a time since we've come back from the hospital. When he's at his loudest, I can hear both the cry through the monitor and his real cry from the room, the screams layered as if there were two babies.

He's looking at me at the moment. I've come back upstairs. His eyes are on me, and he seems satisfied, now that I've come to check on him. I hope he realises that I am doing the best I can. There's a hum in the air, maybe from the washing machine downstairs. I've got a damp cloth in my hand and I run it over the windowsill, the dust felting together into a dark mass of hair and debris.

I should try to feed him, again.

I sit down on the bed and unbutton my shirt, then unhook the clip of the bra, exposing my breast to the air. I put the baby to my nipple which feels raw and tender. He doesn't seem to notice my breast in his face, but I encourage him by rubbing my nipple over his lips and nose, like they show you how to do in the hospital, and it seems to do the trick, as his mouth opens automatically. The feeling disgusts me: to have his little mouth clamped over my areola, his tongue thrusting against my nipple. The letdown comes through and I try not to cry out with the pain. He sucks the point gently, so softly, and I try to think of something else, to wriggle away from the feeling, to think of him not being on my body like this.

Then.

He bites. A searing pain.

But, he doesn't have teeth.

I manage to put my finger into his mouth, to prise him off my nipple. My breast throbs. It takes me a few seconds to unhook his clamped jaw. I have to apply a little more force than I thought I would. His jaw releases with a little click and a wet, sucking *moosh* sound. Milk spurts out from my nipple all over his face and he squeals with rage. My entire breast sings with pain.

It must have been his gums.

I try to put him on the other breast. He refuses, by clamping his mouth shut and moving his head away. I am relieved, and put him down in the basket. The bitten nipple feels exposed. I cover myself.

I'll try again later.

It's just a little thing, and maybe it's only in my head because everything is so overwhelming, but sometimes I've seen him looking at his fingers, and he's intently focused, completely absorbed. Newborn babies aren't meant to be able to focus on things, but he definitely can, I'm sure of it. Maybe he's just a particularly self-aware baby, maybe it's a good thing, I don't know.

In the late afternoon I take the baby out into the garden for a little while, to get some fresh air. See? I say to him, rocking him in my arms. I point out the moors, then the hillock to the right, with its tall pine trees and a few sheep grazing on its slope. Apart from the small disturbance of a clamour of rooks, flitting between the uppermost branches of the pines, it is quiet and still. I can hear myself and the baby breathing, his breathing a little faster than mine. I can see that it has been a beautiful day. I want to stand there for longer, I wish I could, but then the baby begins to cry, until I take him back indoors.

Seònaid MacKay studied graphic design and illustration, at both Glasgow School of Art and the Royal College of Art. Before coming to UEA, she worked as a graphic designer and director for television. She currently lives in London and is writing a collection of short stories.

Sarah Marsh

Marks in the Snow

I was born in the snow. It started falling when my mother was walking along the lanes, concealing the land, until she no longer recognised where she was. I slipped out and landed in the snow, while she sprung forwards, unburdened, and leapt away. She joined a galloping herd of deer, light-footed and free. I was left sprawling in a drift, mottled and blue. The snow covered me, erased me as soon as I was born.

For years, I was troubled by the snow, however lightly it fell. The world became a dreamscape into which I slipped. Occasionally, I would spot litter in the whiteness – a wrapper, a can, some orange peel – and I would bend down and pick it up. Their colour and shape were precious features and I held them close.

The woman who raised me saw me as a space to fill. When I was young, and we lived in a town called X, she would put me in the car, and we would drive to the place where I was born. She would point out the exact spot where I was found, and tell me how the small mound was like a pregnant stomach, one small pink arm sticking out as though my mother, before leaving, had marked the place with a twig. 'A snow child,' she would say. 'She wanted me to find you.'

In the summer holidays, we drove across the country and found beaches tucked into the coves like curved bones. We walked for miles, picking up shells and stones and clumps of seaweed. Back in her cottage, with the quiet road outside, she showed me photographs, put postcards on my walls, and described places she had travelled to as a child. But nothing ever stuck. The pictures entered my thoughts, twitched for a moment, and died.

The doctors looked in my ears. They looked in my eyes. They checked my throat. They checked my heart. They ran memory tests and concluded all was normal. I heard the woman talking to them as I waited outside the consulting room. 'She's missing something. She's not normal at all.' 'She's alive,' they replied. 'Everything ticks.'

Tick.

A snow child, skin pale and hair so blonde it was almost the same colour as the pages in my school books. Later, at university, I tried punctuating the blankness with jewels. I wore red stones around my neck and hung strings of lapis lazuli from my lobes. I took a hot needle and ink and drew ragged swirls up my legs. I wore colours and clashed stripes with paisley. I even began wearing pictures. Pictures of blue forests, metallic cities, and a brown delta stroked by shiny fingers of water. I cut them out of magazines and crammed them into my pockets. I filled my hat and placed it on my head. I could feel the scratch of the paper against my scalp. Wherever I went, the air rustled around me, as though the scraps in my pockets were breathing.

After university, I worked as a cartographer. I spent the weekdays in an office with three wilting pot plants and focused on the computer screen. I made data visual, carefully choosing traits to be mapped while eliminating those characteristics that were not relevant. At the weekends, I travelled to places around the country, to any odd name that might stand out on a map. I was drawn to them like the bright scraps of litter in the snow or the pictures I had selected to put in my pockets. I drew up my own maps and filed them away in cabinets.

The woman who raised me was older now, and moved around the house as though every piece of furniture were a mountain to be navigated. Whenever I returned, she would sit smiling at me, her thoughts moving slowly around in her eyes like silt in a muddy river. But she spoke less now, happy to watch as I sat at the kitchen table drawing maps that orchestrated strange personal elements, a pictorial language that was my own.

I travelled abroad for a while, crossing vast tracts of tundra on a short-necked pony, but an odd sickness took hold of me, and after only six months, I went home to X. The house was muted with sterile shades. I could hear the radiators ticking.

I always returned to X, save for one brief interlude when I married a man who I saw one night on the roadside. My car headlights picked him out, a stocky figure standing in front of some birch trees, straight-backed and silver like the trunks behind him. His thumb was stuck out, and he was wrapped up in seal-grey clothes, the lettering on his T-shirt sharply visible. I stopped the car, empty-headed, and he climbed in. We drove in silence for a while, and then, as though sensing the absence he had entered, he started talking, recounting his journey, telling me how bulls had chased him over a viaduct. His face was warm and the roundness of his figure fitted all the hollows in mine. We had three happy years living in a windmill in a shining city. When the marriage finished, I took to the road again.

Back in X, the woman who had raised me was older still. She was no longer able to move very easily. She sat in a chair in the kitchen and watched me. The next winter, it snowed for seven days. The old emptiness returned. I went out into the snow and began picking up scraps of litter again.

In the following months, I dreamed obsessively about deer, sometimes waking up in the night in a cold sweat. When I shut my eyes again, I would see a woman running among the herd, leaping for the horizon. I saw a snow-covered field and black scratchy trees. The deer were hurtling along the rim, and the sun had just broken through the clouds, sending down fine beams like transparent gold wires. She was there too, running, her skirts flying around her.

I continued travelling around the country but always came back to X. One Autumn, snow fell early, and I sat at the window looking at the trees and the inch of snow laid thickly on their branches. Sometimes I went into town, where the people moved around me like blobs of ink, but mostly I stayed in indoors.

The woman who raised me could be found in various places, sometimes sitting by the fire in the sitting room, or else at the table in the kitchen. A few times she wrapped herself up in blankets, moved slowly outside, and sat on the garden bench in the snow. One morning, I saw her sitting there, unmoving, silent, and was suddenly thrown into a frenzy of anger. I pulled on my coat and went outside, my feet crunching clean footprints across the lawn. I sat down on the bench, and tried to control my breathing, the cold air creeping into my lungs. She sat quietly, smiling, one hand slowly reaching out and patting my knee. I ignored her hand, and said, 'Tell me where I come from.'

She didn't move. I wanted to rattle her, to shake her, to make something come out of her mouth, even if it was no more true than anything else I had ever thought or heard. Her lips parted, the corners ungluing, but no words came. Eventually, she pointed at the apple tree and said, 'Twig.' I got up and crossed over to the tree. Around me, the snow was jewelled with red apples shaken from the branches, the shine taken from their skins by a layer of frost. Instinctively, I wanted to pick one up, and put it in my pocket, but instead I snapped a small branch from the tree. I returned to the bench, and she took the stick from me, carefully, her thick fingers clasping one end. She reached down and drew a mark in the snow. It was clumsily drawn, rudimentary, like an ancient beginning. I looked at it for a while, and then at her. Her eyes were fixed serenely on me but her expression meant nothing. She was too old for my questions now. I stood up and ran inside, slamming doors, throwing myself on the bed, beating pillows.

Two days later, she died in the garden, a frozen tear hanging from the tip of her nose. She was buried in the cemetery in X, a place where names have been rubbed away, and the gravestones are lined up as if marching into the distance.

Every day, I went to her grave. I got down on my knees, pushed my fingers into the soil and cried. When I returned to the house, which was now mine, I began renovating. I removed the furniture, stripped the walls, and painted them the same colour as the snow outside. I bleached the floor and coated it with floor paint. I hung starched curtains that on snowless days would hide the colours outside. I emptied my cabinets, and threw out all the maps and pictures, and then I threw out the cabinets too.

I worked for days, and I didn't stop, even when everything looked the same, and I could barely make out the doorframes, or the lines where the walls met the floor. I kept painting and threw open the windows to release the chemical smell. I didn't stop when my fingers became stiff with dried paint and the walls were so encrusted the paint began to crack. I didn't stop when the snow blew in through the open windows and began piling around my feet. I didn't stop even as the walls became soft, the floor turned into feathers, and the edges in the house became gentle curves and ridges. I didn't stop until the air had been displaced, and the snow covered me, and then I curled up on the floor and closed my eyes.

Sarah Marsh read Human Sciences at Oxford and spent two years teaching English language and literature at a university in Beijing before coming to UEA. She is writing her first novel.

Gavin McCrea

The Real Me

What I want (for people to see who I really am) isn't unusual. What I want (for my face to stop talking for me) (for my breasts) (my arse) (my legs) (to give way to what's underneath) isn't any different to what most women want. What I want (to be uncovered) (to stand as the barest) (truest) (thing) isn't anything to be ashamed of. What I want (to not want anything) (to live wantlessly) isn't easily gained. But perseverance is the secret to success, and recently I got my first taste.

In the end, it came unexpectedly. Nothing about that day prepared me for it. It was a Wednesday (same as Tuesday) (same as Thursday) (I get through them) (one gram) (one milligram) (at a time) and I was in the living room. I was holding a glass. A headache tablet fizzed in the water. Dad was lying on the couch. His jacket and tie were still on. Two of his fingers were pinching the bridge of his nose. A third finger (his other hand) was pointing at the window (it means I have to close the curtains). I moved in the direction his finger was pointing (he doesn't want the light) (it's the light that's giving him the headache) (the light from the late sun) and tried to concentrate on what he was saying (come on) (Sarah) (it might be something you need to remember).

Then I dropped the glass. Actually, I could have sworn it dropped me (freed itself from my grip) (pushed me away). Dad looked annoyed. His mouth was opening wider than before, and closing faster, but I couldn't hear the sound that came from it. There was a flash (not blinding) (but shining) and the solid things stepped away from me (the couch) (the armchair) (the television) (the coffee table) (the treadmill) (the ab-master) and the corners of the room became round (no surprise) (the world is) (after all) and I could feel it (a lightness beneath me) (a breeze blowing up through my bones) and I lay back onto it (yes) and it held me (yes) and lifted me (yes) high enough (yes) (yes) to touch the (—)

But then there was darkness (fell) and heaviness (falling) and I woke up (fallen).

I'd never been there before but I knew where I was (it's Saint Vincent's hospital) (it's Saint Teresa's ward) (the home for broken angels). And I'd never felt it before but I knew what the feeling in my nose and throat was (it's a tube) (reaching down) (putting stones in my belly) (so that I'll stay sunk) (grounded) (drowned-ed). And I'd never seen them before but I knew who the people in the other beds were (it's them) (it's us). I caught their eyes as they moved from the floor, to the wall, to the television and I saw failure in them (my god) (their eyes) but also new determination (we will rise again) (only higher).

Dad was there (for me) when I woke. He'd got off the couch (for me) and called an ambulance (for me) and got back into his car (for me) and followed the ambulance (for me) (for me) (for me). He was pacing the room (up) (down) and I was sure (up) all of this (down) was giving him a terrible headache. He stopped and looked at me in the eyes (his were red) (mine were) (oh god). He went out and didn't come back until the next morning.

He brought my younger brothers with him this time. All three of them were wearing tracksuits (I'm staring) (I can't help myself) (little bulges where their). Dad drew the curtain around us. Your brothers have exams coming up so they won't be able to visit you every day. All of them stood, none of them sat down, the chairs by the bed stayed empty. And I have to work, remember. I can't just drop everything. I'll come as often as I can. I looked at them (the empty chairs) and started to cry.

When they went, they left the curtain drawn and I had nothing to look at (hundreds) (thousands of breaths) (in) (out) (in) (out) (in) (out) until the nurse came and pulled it back, the sound of the metal rings sliding along the bar (Sarah) (don't scrape your knife on your). Please don't close them again (I want to say) I've nothing to hide.

The nurse was nice (in a country way). How are we feeling? (she says) (we) (but I know she means) (me). She attached a new bag to my tube (a

Gavin McCrea

thousand calories) (a moment on the) (a lifetime on the) and tucked in my blanket and put some magazines on the bedside table. You're in the right place, love. All you should worry about is getting your strength back. You're the weak one (I want to say).

The woman in the bed opposite was knitting. I watched her (click) (clack) (click) (clack) (click) (clack) until the lights on the ceiling turned themselves on, and the sky through the window turned itself black, and she disappeared behind the curtain again.

Dad sat down this time. Put his hand on the mattress. Took the sheets in his fist. Squeezed them. Sarah, listen to me (I think just by listening) things are stressful enough (I can tell when) without your mother (the knitting woman) and now you start this (misses a stitch). Sarah, listen to me (I wonder) we're all trying to cope (when) you have to learn to cope too (someone) so please stop this (is going to) if not for yourself (ask me) then for me (what I want).

The mornings started early (television on) and the nights came slowly (television off) but the days passed quickly (on/off) (on/off). I learned the routines of the other women (girls actually) (most of them) (except the knitter) (she's older) (but she doesn't talk) (just knits) (click) (clack). They came to my bed between feeds and shared their stories (once upon a) (there lived a) (happily ever) and I shared mine. The mystery of it (and they nod). The force of it (and they smile). The bliss of it (and they look around to see if the nurse is coming). The freedom of it (and they take my hand) (and they understand) (and they're the same) (and it's what they want too).

And then I was home again (forty-seven kilograms) (of cheek) (of belly) (of thigh). The knitter (she doesn't speak to me for my whole stay) (and then she) gave me a card on my last day, slipped it to me as I sat and waited for Dad to collect me. I put it in a drawer in my bedroom, and from then on, took it out twice a day, once when I woke up and again before I went to sleep (dear friend) (be your own master) (nothing but your own power will keep you going) (you need nothing) (triumph over the need) (with love).

I went back to university. Dad had notified the college administration. Extensions had been granted on my essays. A note had been added to my file. My professor asked to see me. Sarah (I can smell) you look (the excess) well (on her breath).

Dad sent me to a therapist (the best that money can buy) (anything for my angel). The therapist didn't say anything. He just sat there looking at me, waiting for me to start. I promised myself not to (start) (middle) (end) until he asked me (what?) until he asked me (what?) until he asked me (what?) (I want).

I met an old friend from school. Dad found her name in my phone, remembered her from study nights and disco runs. You need friends, Sarah. You need to socialise. He told her everything. I could just imagine her reaction (oh my god) (Mr) (I mean) (that's like) (oh my god) (thanks for letting me know) (Mr). We met in a café in town. Dad drove me in, watched me until I'd gone in the door. He parked in a multi-storey and (knowing him) listened to his opera CDs while he waited. Oh my god, Sarah, like wow, it's been so long. I ordered hot chocolate fudge cake. Cream or ice cream? Both please. I ate the whole thing (wow) (I mean) (oh my god) barely stopping to (in) (out) swallow.

Sometimes after lectures I went to visit the girls in the hospital. The last time I went, the only person I recognised was the knitter (click) (clack) but she didn't acknowledge me (click) (clack) just continued knitting (click) (clack). I sat in one of her chairs and watched some television (reality) (my fat arse) and left.

It didn't take long for Dad and my brothers to think things had got back to normal. In the morning, they saw me leave for university, books and folders under my arm (just like) (nothing) (had happened) and in the evening they saw me cooking in the kitchen (fish noodle soup) (mushroom risotto) (Chinese-style pork) (aubergine lasagne) (baked onion) (chicory salad) (just like) (nothing) (had happened) (to her). Aren't we lucky to have such a good cook in the house? Say thank you to your sister, boys.

Everyone looked relieved all the time. My brothers could sit in the same room as me without trying to avoid looking at me (it's her eyes) (that's how you can really tell) and Dad didn't have to worry about uncomfortable conversations on the golf course (she's grand) (doing great) (thanks be to)

Dad. He's right. I'm doing great (no thanks to him). To thank him, I stop off at the supermarket on the way home from university, buy the

Gavin McCrea

ingredients for a special dinner, and spend all afternoon preparing it.

My brothers come home (they stink of cigarette smoke and deodorant). What's all this? It's nothing. Go change out of your uniforms and help me set the table. Dad rings and says he'll be late. The boys hover around me. We're starving, do we have to wait? Yes, you have to wait. Eat something to keep you going. They wander off with a bowl of olives. I sit at the end of the table with a dishcloth on my lap.

Dad finally comes through the door, pulling off his tie, unbuttoning his shirt. Jesus, what a (etc). I have such a splitting (etc). Something smells (etc). Thanks for doing that Sarah, I don't know what I'd (etc).

We eat. Dad talks with his mouth full (about his job) (he thinks it's going to send him to an early grave) but if I focus on the knives and forks (click) (clack) it's almost like he's not talking at all (click) (clack). Finally, one brother burps and the other laughs. Dad stops talking and frowns. This is my chance (now or)

I'm thinking of moving out.

My brothers look at Dad. Dad looks back at them. They all look at me. Moving out? Yeah (dear friend) I'm thinking of getting a flat (be your own master). Is that such a good idea? It's time I lived by myself (nothing but your own power will keep you going). So soon? Is that wise? I've found a place in town (you need nothing). Let me talk to the doctors. It's just a bedsit but I like it (triumph over the need). Can I have your room if you go? Yes, take it (with love).

Dad sighs. My brothers look at their plates. Dad gets up. Where are the headache tablets? There's a new box in the cupboard. We all watch the tablets dissolve in the glass. Bubbles rising. Then gulped down. Dad wipes his mouth with the back of his hand. Sarah (yes). Sarah (I'm here). Sarah (look under the forty-seven kilograms) (and you'll find me). Sarah (waiting) (patiently) (for new successes). Sarah (yes) (yes) I'm talking to you. Yes? Is this really what you want?

Gavin McCrea was born and educated in Dublin. 'The Real Me' is from the collection *But You Can't Touch*. He is currently working on a novel entitled *An Honest Woman*.

Priscilla Morris

The Intruders
An extract from a novel-in-progress

It was a couple of weeks before war broke out and the streets of Sarajevo were filling with strange faces; coarse, ugly faces that did not fit. I pulled my coat tighter and hurried through town on my way to the studio. As I walked, I heard the harsh peasant dialects of mountain villages and the slang of the streets and the prisons. The rumour was spreading that all the criminals had been released from jail to defend the city against the troops that were gathering in the hills. To defend the city against the troops gathering in the hills, people were saying. There was a looseness to the atmosphere. Deutschmarks flashed everywhere.

A phone call.
My wife, Sonja, answered it and turned pale.
'That was Gordana,' she said. 'A family of bandits has broken into Mum's flat. She's called the police, but they won't leave. Get your coat. We must go at once!'
Emilija, my mother-in-law, had been living with us since the previous autumn. She was eighty-nine, ill and frail; hardly able to dress or feed herself. Her apartment, Sonja's childhood home, was in a good mansion block on a tree-lined street in Old Sarajevo. I had painted it twice. Once from the living room looking out through open doors: a bowl of pomegranates and split-open figs on the table in the foreground, and once from the street: a tall yellow building with trees brushing up against it, a glimpse of inner courtyard in deep violet shadow through a wide archway. It was full of antique books and fine furniture. My insides

tightened at the thought of strangers being there, fingering the beautiful objects.

We pulled on our coats and caught the trolley, then the tram, across town in silence. It must have been late March but it was still as cold as winter. The cherry trees along the Miljacka were holding back their blossom in tight white fists and the waters of the river were a churned-up brown, swollen with rain and melted snow. Sleet slapped our faces as we got off the tram and ran down our necks in icy trickles. Our toes started to numb as we picked our way through the slush, so that by the time we stood outside Emilija's flat we were wet through and frozen, stones of dread in our stomachs. We were not young; we had never been fighters.

I rang the bell.

A bored-looking policeman answered, toothpick jutting from his mouth. Without taking it out or saying a word, he cocked his head to one side to direct us through to the living room. Sonja gripped my arm as we pushed past him. Two pairs of grey trainers and a pair of scuffed court shoes were lined up beneath the hall mirror.

In the living room of my mother-in-law's flat, a second policeman stood, hands in pockets. Two tall men in their twenties were lounging on chairs. A fire had been lit in the stove and the younger of the two was leaning over to prod it with a poker. The other had his back to us and was rocking in his chair, his feet kicked up on Emilija's tasselled sofa, sitting plum in the middle of which was a large-chested woman in her late fifties, or thereabouts. Her black hair was pulled up into a high bun and she had a spot of rouge on the middle of each cheek. She was so short that her feet did not touch the floor, but she sat up straight-backed and regal as Queen Sissi of Hungary. All three were smoking, a carton of American cigarettes ripped open on the coffee table, ash flaking onto the floor.

Sonja and I stared at the intruders, ice melting into our coats.

'What are you doing here?' I asked, my voice higher than usual.

The man with his back to us swivelled his head round and sneered. He looked like a tiger. He had a flat face, a square jaw and an intense orange hue to his skin. His eyes flashed arrogantly. We found out later that he was, in fact, one of the many petty criminals released from jail around that time. He had been imprisoned for holding up tobacconist shops.

'We've moved in,' the short woman answered.

'But this is my mother-in-law's flat,' I said. 'You can't just move in.'

'We can if the flat's deserted,' the woman said slowly. 'Or the owner dead.'

Sonja tightened her grip on my arm. The younger man, who had started whittling splints of wood to add to the fire, glanced up through hair that drooped over his face, but said nothing.

'Don't be ridiculous,' I said.

She reached forwards to drag a finger across the coffee table, and then held it up for us to see.

'Look at the dust in this place,' she said. 'No one's lived here for months, years even. This is the flat of a dead woman. I *know* it.'

I looked round for the policeman, but he had slipped outside to join his colleague.

'We're not going anywhere unless you can prove her mother's alive,' said the woman, jerking her head towards Sonja.

'Of course, my mother's alive,' Sonja burst out. 'She's living with us right now.'

A smile as smug as a camel's appeared on Queen Sissi's lips.

'She's dead.'

'She's not!'

'Well, my dear, we won't go till you bring her to us.'

We went outside to ask the policemen for help, but they shrugged and looked blank-faced. Furious, we hurried to the nearest police station to make a report. No one seemed interested. There was a feeling of waiting; of killing time.

Finally, a policeman looked up from the game of cards he was playing to say: 'Look, the rich are all leaving the city, getting out while they can. The council's said all empty flats are up for grabs.'

'But that's absurd,' I said. 'We have the deeds in a drawer somewhere. Surely you can do something.'

'Like what?' the policeman asked. 'No one's in charge here.' He slapped the chest of his national police uniform. 'And who knows how much longer we're going to be wearing these for,' he added, before turning his back on us and resuming his card game.

The only course of action, it seemed, was to go home and bring my mother-in-law to the flat. She had not been outside the whole winter and was alarmed when Sonja and the maid tried to squeeze her feet into her shoes. She thought we were trying to get rid of her. 'Why must I go to my flat?' she kept saying. 'Don't you want me here? I'm too ill to live alone. It's snowing outside!'

I went to persuade a taxi-driver who lived on our street to drive us to Old Sarajevo. Emilija was far too weak to use trams and trolleys.

It was dark when we got there. We rang the bell and the younger son let us in, the policemen having long gone. Sonja and I guided my mother-in-law into the living room, where the lamps had been lit and the curtains drawn. The younger son went over to the stove to feed the fire. The elder son had moved onto the sofa next to his mother. She seemed not to have moved at all, other than to lay a heavily-ringed hand on her son's knee. The two of them were speaking quietly, each holding a cut glass tumbler full of amber liquid in one hand. Their eyes rose to stare at us flatly as we entered.

My mother-in-law gasped on seeing them and pulled away from our supporting hands. She took a shaky step towards the orange circle that the open stove was throwing over the three intruders.

'Who are they?' she asked, peering short-sightedly at the trio, like a toddler intrigued and confused by something out of place.

The three intruders froze as if they had seen a ghost: they must have really believed we had been lying to them. The colour drained from Queen Sissi's face, leaving the two red dots of rouge glowing like embers on her cheeks. Her sons turned to her, a twitch working under tiger face's right eye.

'Who are they?' Emilija repeated, her voice quivering.

The large-chested woman jumped up from the sofa, pushed past my mother-in-law and came up to Sonja and me. She was barely taller than a child, but her sons got up at the same time and stood behind her, flanking her like giant playground bullies.

'All right,' she said grandly, as if granting us a favour. 'All right. We'll leave now.'

It took less than five minutes for them to gather their bags and jackets. The woman nodded to her elder son and he scooped up several bottles of whiskey, vodka and slivovitz from Emilija's drinks cabinet.

As they were leaving, she turned to Sonja, and said with a leer, alcohol hot on her breath: "Just remember this, my dear: your mother's flat is not safe. Don't think it will stay empty. Other people who come – *and they will come* – won't leave so easily."

Emilija crossed over to the sofa and perched on its edge. Sonja and I remained uncertainly in the centre of the room, staring out of the door the intruders had just left open.

That was our first sign of the anarchy that lay around the corner.

Priscilla Morris read Anthropology at Jesus College, Cambridge, and has taught English in Spain and Brazil. She won the UEA *Seth Donaldson Memorial Bursary* in 2008. She is writing a novel inspired by the story of her great uncle, a Bosnian Serb painter whose life's work burnt down during the siege of Sarajevo.

Jack Reynolds

Void

The following is an edited extract from Void, a novel

I would never have come here if Barclays hadn't tracked me down at my last place. I left with £72 and the promise of a landscaping job, ready to start up again, only to find that an influx of migrant workers had cut labouring pay in half. The last work in the city's for the Council Cleansing Department, and to get that I had to sign a waiver saying I'd accept £1.26 an hour less than the minimum wage, which I didn't think was legal. The only reason I can even get a look in there is because the Council can't deal directly with the gangmasters. They have to go through an agency, and they don't care who they send, as long as they can cream off their precious £1.26 an hour. So six days a week I get up at 4:30 and cycle for an hour to be first in line at the allocation window, ahead of the Poles.

Now that I'm on the void team it's not so bad. If the team you're with files a request for you – like George always does for me – and you're in the queue next morning at 5:30, then you can be sure of work every day, but if you're even five minutes late the form becomes worthless, and you're back jostling at the window for the last place on the litterpicking team. Men cry and beg at that window. There's never more than twenty men needed, and sometimes as few as five, but every day the agency sends ten, and the King of Poland's van holds another sixteen. Tony's girlfriend Tracy works behind the window at the sandwich factory on the other side of the industrial estate. It's worse there. She has to deal with whole crying families holding babies up to the glass.

I used to have to walk in, but Tony let me pick a bike from one of the voided lockups he's managed to lose in the system – part of an illicit storage network that reaches all the way round the ring road. Everyone says that if you need a fridge, a cooker or a TV then Tony's got one stashed within half a mile of your house. It's a good bike, now that I've had some time to work on it. I used up a roll of gaffa tape making some new handgrips and padding the saddle with a folded tea towel, and scrubbed and lubricated its workings with vegetable oil to get rid of most of the surface rust. I only have access to seven of the twenty-three gears, but they're the best ones, so it's no real loss.

This morning it's performing well – the chain's stayed on and I'm in plenty of time. I'm asleep for most of the journey to work, only half-registering the landmarks I pass, the abandoned Shell garage that's been turned into a hand carwash, the block of sheltered housing opposite the park, the porn shop clad in blue-painted chipboard. The dark sky beyond the ring road gives me the feeling that I'm actually cycling home to bed, but soon I cross the road by the Polar Street roundabout, into the industrial estate and towards the dawn. By the time I'm at the depot the sun's made progress and the sky is light, though the streetlights are still on.

My bike-lock's rusted shut, so I ride past the front gate to the trees that shelter the depot from the noise and dirt of the ring road traffic, where there are some rhododendron bushes I can hide the bike in. I scramble up the fence and drop into the car park behind the control building. The King of Poland's rusty white van is on the other side of the loading bays, his men spilling out of the side door like guts from a sheep. From what I've heard he sleeps eight to a room and charges £50 a week each, then takes another £40 for his services. He's got them all lined up now, making sure that those who didn't get a shift yesterday are first at the window today.

Round the front of the control building the contract guys are hanging about smoking duty free fags and drinking from plastic cups. Maisie's behind the plexiglass today, and despite the purple, bubbling skin disorder that covers half her face, she's cheerful.

    Morning duck. What's your number?
    4542. There should be a form in.
    She flicks half-heartedly through a sheaf of thin paper.

Jack Reynolds

Let's see, 4542, 4542, no, nothing for 4542.

It's there. I watched George put it in the slot.

It's definitely there. It's for George, Team 20.

Is your name Carl?

Yeah.

He's put your name on instead of your number. I'll let it through for today, but make sure he does it right tomorrow. Know where you're going?

Yeah. Thanks.

I get away from the window just before it's overrun by the Poles. They shout and push, and don't use the British system of queuing, but there's still a system at work. They all know who's next, and if anyone cuts ahead, they will be pushed to the back. Since it serves no use, and seems to confuse what should be a simple process, I've started to think that the swarming and shouting's a ploy. I think they reckon that if they're unruly enough Maisie'll just get flustered and give them all a shift. It never works. One by one they go over to the kerb and have their morning drink. They all drink at least one can of cheap lager before starting work, seated in a line on Primark fleeces in front of the control building, smoking dusty West Red cigarettes. I don't blame them, but I couldn't face it. It's so early I can't even think about smoking without my chest getting tight. At this time in the morning my whole respiratory system is bathing in phlegm, repairing itself from the day before. Only when I feel it has regenerated enough do I light up, usually about 9:00.

The void team trucks are parked near the gate, well away from the control building. Voiding is the best job here. The void teams don't have to wait in line to check a van out of the depot, and George and Tony even get to take theirs home. Tony's is an ancient Ford flatbed with a new yellow paintjob and a red cage on the back like the rest of the council vans, and he's not really supposed to take it home, but George has an eighteen-ton twelve-wheeled Scania, bought new last year. He's the only one who's ever driven it. He gets it because he lives by the maintenance depot on the other side of the ring road, so he can bring in parts to the repair shop on his way to work. He loves the truck. He's glued strips of doormat to the footplates so we can wipe our feet before entering the cab.

The passenger door's open, waiting for me, and when I pull myself up

and in I find George rolling his fags for the day and listening to his rockabilly tape. I sling my lunch under the seat, sit down and shut the door. George doesn't like it to be slammed, and he nods approvingly at my light touch. His face is always a shock. He looks like a gargoyle doorknocker missing its iron ring – his nose almost meets his chin, and somewhere in the central crease is a tiny mouth only locatable by a thin handlebar moustache. He's sixty-two, tall, with a rangy, spry set to his joints and powerful, tattooed forearms. Sitting doesn't seem natural to him – he always looks uncomfortably compressed like one of the snakes that fly out of those trick jars of nuts and put kids' eyes out. He finishes rolling and turns the music off.
 Morning.
 Morning.
 Form in all right?
 You left my number off, but yeah, it was there.
 What's your number again?
 4542.
 George nods. I put the music back on. George screws a fag into his face and I turn up the volume – my favourite song on the tape is next.
 At the Polar Street roundabout George turns toward Ingleside and the city fills the windscreen. I once read somewhere that sunlight is the best disinfectant, but that doesn't seem to be true, at least not in the real world. The rising sun just makes the black stains on the grey buildings more stark, a reminder that this is a place of freezing rain and creeping mould, that a day like today should be considered an anomaly, that normal service will be resumed shortly. George doesn't work before 8:00. He says they don't pay him enough, and if his £13,000 a year isn't enough, then my £4.12 an hour definitely isn't. For two and a half hours every morning we sit in the Ingleside community centre café with his wife Linda, who's the cleaner there. It doesn't open till 10:00, and it's got an L-shaped delivery bay where we can hide the truck, so we're safe.
 The community centre's heating is always turned right up and today, as usual, I'm drowsy as soon as I sit on one of the grey plastic chairs. Linda brings us the papers from reception and George makes tea. It's his turn. Linda sits next to me with a copy of *Let's Talk!* magazine. She draws my attention to a story about a middle-aged woman who'd lost her heart and her savings to a Turkish waiter.

Jack Reynolds

They tracked him down too – listen: 'Pamela was an old woman who was sad and wanted sex. I was a gigolo. It was a difficult time in my life and I did many things that I am not proud of, but I am not a thief. I did not steal from her. Pam understood the arrangement. I have a wife now.'

I try to adopt the right expression of leering revulsion. Linda raises her pencilled-on eyebrows.

They only do it up the arse, you know, the Turks.

What?

It's true – they won't do it normally until they get married.

I nod slowly as if this confirms long-held suspicions about the Turks, and flick through the papers. Linda has nothing more to add. George brings the tea over, turns the radio on to 103.6, the local talk station, unclips the walkie-talkie from his belt and gets a Frederick Forsyth out of his bag. The papers are empty. I give up on them, shut my eyes and listen to an argument about Muslims on the radio.

I wake up. The clock above the stand full of self-help leaflets says 9:26. George and Linda's heads are nodded like powered-down robots. The walkie-talkie chatters on low volume. I'm considering how to go about waking George, but he does it himself, turning to look at the clock and grimacing. He turns up the volume knob.

-ing, George? 626 from control 626 from control, receiving?

Hi Maisie, what is it?

I've been trying to get you for twenty minutes.

George runs a hand through his oiled hair.

I was having a shit.

Maisie laughs, George winks at me.

Thanks for that. Got a void for you – dead smackhead in Hodridge, police have just signed off on it. Got to be done by close of play this afternoon.

Why the rush?

Don't ask me, I'm just passing it on. You know where you're going?

Yep. Over and out.

Over and out duck.

Jack Reynolds was born in Great Yarmouth, and is currently completing his first novel, *Void*, and a collection of short stories about time travel, *They Will Send For You Someday*. After graduating from UEA he plans to work and write in London.

Jacob Rollinson

Hastings

Judith had been talking about how much she looked forward to the lock-in all week, but when it finally came around, she just cried for hours. Nobody could make her stop. Beth sat with her for a while, and bought her a drink. Rob said she was being hysterical.

'Why does she have to be so hysterical?' he asked Sam. Sam, who was tending the bar, didn't know. He poured them each a pint of beer. Rob looked up over Sam's head, frowned, and pointed to a spot on the wall above the spirit display. 'Where's the photo of Tommy gone?' he asked.

'It fell down on Monday,' Sam said, 'the frame broke, so I'm getting it fixed.' Rob nodded. 'The picture's fine.' Rob nodded again. They drank their beer.

'Good old boy, Tommy,' said Rob.

'None better.'

A lot of the old gang from The Hastings was there. Davy was there, and Justin, and Pete. Beth had brought her cousin Sarah, and some bloke called Ramon who stood by the jukebox in a big leather jacket, and there were a couple of local regulars who'd managed to escape chuck-out time. And Chris was there, and Steve, and Mac and Sally. But Paul hadn't come in with Judith tonight, and she wouldn't stop crying.

'Where's the photo of Tommy?' asked Mac.

'It fell down. It's getting fixed,' Sam said. Mac nodded. Then he turned, quite deliberately, and looked at Rob. He looked hard at him. Rob kept his own gaze carefully fixed on the surface of the bar.

'How's your cousin?' Mac asked.

'He'll be all right,' Rob replied.
'Yes?'
'Yeah.'
'Good old boy,' Mac said. He made his way back to his table, stopping to pat Judith on the head; she shook his hand off and Beth shooed him away. Mac chuckled to himself. Rob raised his eyebrows at Sam; Sam, pouring another drink, stayed neutral.
People came and went.
'Where's Tommy?' asked Steve.
'Getting fixed. The frame broke.'
'Good old boy.'
People came and went, but Rob hung close to the bar. 'Do you remember the last lock-in we had at The Hastings?' he asked. Sam smiled. He did. 'Everyone kept asking Sharon if it was closing down. And she kept saying no way, not a chance –'
'And she'd already sold all the optics and the till –'
'– and half the chairs. But she was having none of it.'
Sam watched Rob shift his shoulders and face into position, ready to repeat his well-practised impersonation of the woman. 'I dunno wha is all about? It's loik summun *tarks* to summun else un they *tark* to summun else ... it's loik *choinese whiskers!*'
Sam laughed obligingly, looking down, conscious of Rob's eyes trying to engage him. 'Chinese whiskers,' he enjoined, eventually, and Rob laughed all in a rush and over-loud. Sam could see, just behind him, that Pete had moved up to the bar and was listening with interest.
'Chinese whiskers?' he said, loudly, close enough to Rob's ear to make him jump. Pete chortled and repeated himself, affecting a mocking oriental accent and tugging on an imaginary beard: 'Chinee ... wishkah!' He pulled the edges of his eyes apart and stuck his top row of teeth out, swaying from side to side. Sam and Rob laughed; Rob looked back at Sam.
'Oi, wait –'
Pete broke off and pointed at the spot on the wall above the spirit display. 'Where's Tommy gone?'
Rob answered his question before Sam could.
'He fell down.'

Pete looked at Rob with an expression of exaggerated suspicion.

'Fall down, did he? You didn't go and knock our Tommy off the wall, did you mate? *Our Tommy?*' He pressed a knuckle into Rob's flank. A hard knuckle, half-serious.

And Sam laughed. Rob remained silent.

'How's your cousin?' Pete asked.

'He'll be all right,' Rob replied.

'Good old boy,' said Pete, and – to Sam – 'mind you get that photo up, mate.'

'Good old boy,' said Sam.

'Good old boy.'

After Pete had gone, Sam could hear Judith more clearly, crying over on her table. Beth was still sitting with her, but now she'd started talking to Sarah. Judith had her hands tucked in front of her, her head down, eyes closed. She looked all folded up; embarrassed.

'For fuck's sake,' said Rob. He pulled a small, clear plastic bag out of his jacket pocket, and pulled open its mouth. 'Put your finger in the bag?' he said.

Sam considered it. He sighed, and told Rob he didn't want to let himself in for anything. 'Put your finger in the fucking bag, mate,' said Rob. So Sam put his finger in the bag. He washed the bitter crystals down with beer.

Good old boy.

Mac called over to Ramon to put some music on. Ramon shrugged, and started looking over the jukebox selection. Thirty seconds later, the opening chords of *Hotel California* washed over the room.

'Whatever happened to Sharon,' Sam asked, 'after The Hastings?'

'She'll be all right,' said Rob. 'Ask Mac.' The last two words he said with some venom. He drew his finger through a puddle of beer on the counter. 'I don't know why she has to be so hysterical,' he said.

'Sharon?'

'Her,' he said, indicating Judith.

'What do you know about it?' Sam asked.

'Nothing!' Rob held his hands up: innocent. 'It's just … bloody women … isn't it?'

Sam looked sharp at Rob. 'Why don't you go ask her to put her fucking finger in your bag, mate?' he said.

Rob left the bar. Sam cleaned a few glasses. He chastised himself for speaking out. He was tired, he supposed; out of balance. The back of his head was already feeling warm. He wondered if he'd let himself in for anything. He checked the clock: twelve fifteen.

At twelve thirty, Judith got out of her chair and walked to the Ladies.

At one o'clock, Sam was having difficulty calculating change.

'Come on, boy,' said Davy, 'this is supposed to be a party, waste yourself a fucking drink.'

'Yeah, and waste one for me, too,' said Pete. People laughed. Good old boy, they said. After a few minutes, Sam locked the till and left the bar. He lowered the wooden barrier carefully behind him, checking that his keys were still hanging from their chain on his belt.

The corridor to the bathroom was bright, and quiet, and gently undulating. Through the door to the Ladies, he could hear Judith's voice. She was talking; her voice was gentle and monotonous; no other voice talked back. He paused outside the door until he felt guilty, then stepped past as lightly as he could.

The scent of urinal cakes in the Gents was overwhelming: it was heady, exotic, almost alluring. Sam relieved himself into the trough. As he did so, he could hear Mac and Steve muttering furtively in the cubicle behind. He cleared his throat.

'That you, boy?'

'Yep.'

'Good old boy. Get in here.'

The cubicle lock slid into the vacant position, and Sam squeezed inside. He shut the door after. Steve's gut was pressed against him, and Mac's backside. They both wore bomber jackets, both covered in little tears and burn-holes; they smelled of cigarette smoke.

'You will be putting that photo of Tommy back up, won't you, boy?'

'Yes, mate.'

'Good old boy.'

'Wasn't Tucker meant to be here tonight?' Steve asked.

'Supposed to be.'

'And what about Jonto, and Mary?'

'What about Paul?' Sam asked. The other men said nothing. He continued: 'I mean, Judith –'

But his words were cut off; Mac, banknote in his nostril, lurched over the toilet cistern and sniffed the first of three lines of powder. His backside crushed Sam against the cubicle wall. Steve followed Mac, manoeuvring his mass awkwardly around the others. Steve sniffed hard, and exhaled slowly, and Sam felt the man's body relax as though he were releasing a weight of emotion.

'I don't know,' Steve said, 'seems like every time I turn around, someone's missing.' He handed the note to Sam. 'Remember The Hastings?' he said.

And after Sam had sniffed, and felt the powder running cold down the back of his throat, he replied: 'The Hastings remembers you, mate.' He laughed. The others stared at him; he wondered whether he'd gone too far, then noticed the blood dribbling from his nose.

On the way back to the bar, Mac and Steve caught Rob trying to push his head through the door into the Ladies. Mac pulled him out and kicked him to the floor.

'Get out, you dirty cunt,' he growled.

'You dirty cunt,' said Steve.

Rob started talking but when he saw Sam standing behind the others, he shut his mouth. They let him get up and sidle past, his back to the wall, hands up.

Innocent.

Sam followed the others through to the front, where he could hear the opening chords of *Hotel California* repeating, all warm and golden, like the electric light on the wood-panelled walls. And all the old crew from The Hastings were there, (Sam stumbled as he entered the room) Davy and Justin and Beth and Pete and Sarah, (he rested his drink on a stool) and a big leather jacket, a jukebox, Beth and Pete and Sarah and Tommy – no, not Tommy, but Pete and Sarah certainly – all the old names from The Hastings asking one another, 'Who's missing?', 'Are we winning, mate, are we winning?'

There was broken glass on the floor. The drinking and laughter was accelerating ... to the pace that would carry them all to the morning and beyond, if they really let themselves in for it. Sam had the feeling that they would.

Jacob Rollinson

Pete stood behind the bar, helping himself to a pint. 'I think the Wherry's out, mate,' he told Sam. Sam made no complaint. He opened the trapdoor and lowered himself into the cellar.

It was cool down there. Sam pulled the trapdoor shut behind him, muffling the noise of the bar. Instead, he listened to the gentle hum of the chiller, the rhythmic tap of the pump system. The entire cellar pulsated. He sat down on a barrel and ran a hand through his hair. He remembered The Hastings. It was a shell of bleached words, jaw-tensed greetings and whitewashed morning departures. It was a list of names without faces: good old boys, who'd fought and fallen in the fight against the dawn. They'd really let themselves in for it. By the end, they said, there was so little left it wouldn't even burn down properly. Ask Mac.

Sam shut his eyes and listened to the machines. He wondered if he could hear, behind the lifting and decaying cycles of clicks and whirs, and the fizz of his overheated synapses, something leaking. The lightest of footsteps that never reached the floor. The sweetest sensation, slipping away, unborn.

He wondered whether he was being hysterical.

Jacob Rollinson was born in a converted dairy in Ickworth Park, Suffolk, and spent his childhood on other National Trust estates across England and Northern Ireland. Prior to the Masters, he studied English Literature with Creative Writing at UEA. He now plans to teach English abroad.

Donna Sharpe

Night Light
The beginning of a novel

'It's the end of the world!'

The voice was high with distress. Lucia paused. It had been another long day. All she wanted was the cool dark silence of her office.

'It's the end of the worl-dddd!'

Instead, she turned into Ward B, reaching the new patient's bedside just as his cry crescendoed. He sank back onto his pillows, shaking with effort.

'It's the end of the world,' he whispered.

She looked into his eyes, checking how brightly they were glittering, judging the likelihood of an attack.

'It's all right, George,' she said, feeling for his pulse, deciding to risk simply sitting with him. Holding his wrinkled hand, maintaining eye contact, they breathed in, and breathed out. In. Out. In rhythm, together.

'It's all right, George. See, it's all right.'

He nodded, a slow, unsure inclining of his head. She still felt doubtful about calling him George. He had arrived a week ago, and the hospital still hadn't found any official record of a matching George Harrowby – no trace on the electoral role, at the dole office, or on the NHS system. There had been no visitors, and he had just looked blank when asked for next-of-kin details. The moment for an attack seemed to be passing. In any case, the night nurses were arriving. She could leave George (or Not-George) in their hands. And keep her final, most important appointment of the day.

She felt her body relax as she approached the end of the corridor and the flaked gold lettering on her office door came into focus. Professor Lucia Brooke, Chief Psychiatrist, MA., MBBS., PhD., FRCP. did not lead to a grand consulting room but to a municipally simple cell with pale green walls, a single window and a thin brown carpet. Some of her colleagues made their marks with certificates of achievement, family photos, pictures of pets and the like. She made hers with a large rectangular slab of Portland stone stolen from a nearby building site.

She untied the laces of her brown brogues and pulled them off. Reaching under her beige corduroy skirt, she yanked her tights down so quickly she laddered them, but she didn't care, the only thing she cared about right now was making contact. It was the closest she could get to home these days. And to him.

Stepping onto the ancient limestone, she relished its coolness against her tired flesh. The secret ritual felt luxurious. She looked down at her feet, misshapen by yellowing corns, greying hard skin and the weight of a working life spent standing. Embedded in the slab near her big toe, the one whose ingrowing nail was a mouldering ochre, was the antediluvian curve of a tiny fossil.

Kneeling down, she tenderly traced its outline with her fingertip. He – she – it – must have been immortalised in limestone two hundred million years ago. She laid first her forehead and then her cheek against her old friend, wanting to know how to become that safe, even if it meant being swept from one's natural habitat, calcified in rock for millennia and never, ever feeling anything again.

Swerving to the right, Lucia avoided yet another pothole on Shoreditch High Street. The light was falling now and the orange heads of streetlamps were emerging like giraffes' heads above concrete foliage. She breathed in sharply as a passing car forced her to veer left to escape being flattened. Merging with the rest of the traffic into the Kingsland Road, pedalling harder, faster, she smiled as endorphins flooded her body. Breathing in, she let the fumes fill her lungs. When hints of cardamom and mint seeped in, she slowed down. They heralded her favourite moment of the day.

She got off her bike and pushed it, wanting to prolong the experience, not merely whizz past on wheels. The Turkish grocery was always open, its doorway garlanded by huge bunches of mint, shiny mounds of lemons and sacks of grain piled so high they peaked like snowy mountain ranges. In the café next door, what looked like a whole lamb was roasting on a spit. Glistening browny-red slices were being carved off, laid between oval pouches of bread and parsley, tomato, onion and mint heaped on top.

Men were sitting at crowded tables, sharing piled-high plates of food, puffs of smoke from tubes attached to shiny brass pots and glasses of dark red juice, black coffee and what looked like yoghurt. She stood perfectly still and watched the orange tips of their cigarettes glow behind the glass. The idea that she could step into the café, ask for lamb and bread and salad, then eat with such enjoyment that juices would run down her chin, never occurred to her.

Instead, she got back onto her bicycle and continued north up the Kingsland Road. Past where Turkish turf gave way to West African, past the Geffrye Museum's genteel English garden that looked so foreign, past St Leonard's Hospital with its workhouse whiff seeping like gas through its modern façade. She had to pedal harder to get up the bridge that arched over the canal. An old cobbled ramp built to rescue ponies that fell into the water seemed a personal gift; it made getting her bike onto the towpath so much easier, although the rope grooves were a menace to her wheels. She turned right into the Kingsland Basin. A few paraffin lamps were glowing through thin curtains. Leaving her bike on the jetty, she stepped onto the deck of *Geranium*, the forty-six-foot long narrowboat that was home.

Inside, she sat down on the tartan-covered bunk that did for sofa, bed, chair, everything. Years ago, she had laid a beautiful Persian rug inherited from her father on the floor. Random leaks and the constant tramping in of mud from the towpath had changed it beyond recognition. Above it hung a single shelf, where marked-down tins of food jostled for space with wrenches, nails and a hammer. A little pot-bellied stove sat empty, like a disgruntled deity. A single ring camper stove did for the kitchen, and she could turn it on without getting up. She was down to one of most things, one plate, one knife, one fork, although she did still have two spoons and two mugs. Just one saucepan though. She placed it onto the glowing circle and poured in tomato soup.

Donna Sharpe

It wasn't long before she could spoon the bubbling synthetic liquid into her mouth.

She shut the little door that connected her to the world. The curtains were still as tightly drawn as they had been that morning. Lighting her single lamp, she looked towards a knee-high stack of notebooks at the end of the bunk. The current one lay open on top of the damp and curling paper tower. She picked it up and lay down, the scratchy blanket itching against her skin. With a chewed-up biro, she wrote the date at the top of the next clean page, as she had been doing for years now, and then began.

'Today, we cycled out through the city together, along the towpath, as far east as Limehouse. We both kept blinking in the bright glare of the September sun. An Indian summer would be nice, B. said, smiling at me, kissing me, and I could taste the sun on his lips – '

The heavy nudge of another barge nosing against the boat made her look up. It was only the weight of a neighbour jumping onto their own deck. She returned to her notebook, going deeper and deeper into the details of the day, beginning to relax word by word, to feel that warm glow inside. She leant back against the wood slats that formed an inner wall inside the boat's steel body, and caught a glimpse of herself in the broken mirror.

Her once angular face was now gaunt, her creamy skin grey, her blue eyes accessorised with dark bags of skin. Yet she chose to see the face of a young woman, standing up (she stood up), running towards someone (she shuffled a few steps forward), mouth breaking open in a smile (she gave it a go), arms flung out ready to embrace her lover (she tried, but the narrowness of the barge cut her off). In the shard of glass, she saw her lover running towards her, sweeping her up in a cinema-style embrace as a swirl of steam wrapped its warm grey arms around them both, and the mirror misted over.

The tendrils of soup left in the saucepan were corroding into blackness, burning up. She let the smoke rise and rise, ignoring the acrid smell curling into her nostrils. She imagined the hot dirty haze of a train pulling out at a station; the mist on the canal early in the morning; the roaring black plumes of a direct hit. There, that did it. Her body twitched into life. She slipped her hand up her skirt, under her knicker elastic,

Night Light

over wiry, greying hair. Then retracted it. There was no need to be inside either material or flesh. Pressing down over cotton, she knew she could apply enough pressure to achieve the result she wanted without ever having to touch that little bunched-up bud of flesh and nerves or any other part of her body, inside or out. There had been a time, years ago, when she used to slip her fingers inside that hot, wet part of herself, but she'd found this way was far more – convenient. Much less fuss. No wiping of herself onto sheets, blankets, clothes, no rich smell staying on her fingertips for hours until she washed it off with medical strength disinfectant at the hospital. External pressure mixed with internal – images. That was the recipe for speedy success.

The smoke was threateningly black now, no longer wispy hints of romance but a dark, nearly solid-looking menace growing in intensity. She flipped through her mental card-file of scenarios. Selected one. It did the job. Less than sixty seconds later, her body briefly shuddered as a quick warmth shot through her

Harriet was always trying to get her along to consciousness-raising workshops, Reichian screaming therapy weekends, reclaiming your body days. She simply hadn't had the heart to say that as she was having, on average, three orgasms a day, achieved with surgical speed and precision, she really didn't feel she needed any more help with the matter.

The whole boat was filled with the damned smoke now. Jumping up, she grabbed the offending saucepan from the ring. Pulling open the little door to the main deck, she hurled it into the canal where it bobbed along, sizzling as cold water met hot metal. The smoke that had been trapped inside the boat's tiny interior billowed out into the night air.

Donna Sharpe has written, directed and produced ten documentary films for the BBC, including episodes of the BAFTA-nominated *Who Do You Think You Are?* and the BAFTA-winning *Trouble at the Top*. She has recently finished her first novel *English Gothic*, and is working on her second *Night Light*.

UEA Creative Writing Anthology 2009

Gareth Watkins

Locke

Enough is Enough

My personal life is my personal life, and this site does not exist to discuss it.

I have an unmoderated comments section because free speech remains a right in this country (and will do so right up until Barry Hussein Obama decides that it might hurt somebody's feelings), not to gather up a lot of limp-wristed missives about 'making it through' and 'the grieving process'. No PalinforPrez58, I don't need 'some time alone to work things out': while I'm sure that in California* your organic Native American granola collective will give you a good decade of paid 'personal time' for chanting, colonic irrigation and all other aspects of 'personal growth', here in America we work for a living.

Stick to the issues in the comments section or have them deleted. I'm drawing a line in the sand here.

*As always, criticism of the rogue state of California doesn't imply criticism of governor Schwarzenegger – it takes a lot to corral forty million fags, gang-bangers and illegals into something resembling civilization.

Posted by Locke September 18 2008

Comments (67)

Why Feminists Hate Sarah Palin

Smart, successful, sexy, socially conservative, and the ladies – sorry, *womyn* of the feminist blogosphere can't get enough of her. In the last twenty-four hours Feministing.com (you'll forgive me if I don't link to it) have taken a little time out from their busy schedule (making sure the ads for dildos are prominent enough, cheerleading for Hussein-Obama, planning their next 'Drink till you abort' happy hour) to write three adorably ill-informed posts about how Palin makes them feel, like, all gross and stuff.

Now, I know that the smart and sassy, independent womyn of Feministing (quote: 'I'll admit it: I find the debate over healthcare in America incredibly confusing at times. What I do know is pretty simple.') don't need no man to tell them what to think, but maybe they'd like to chew this over: maybe the reason y'all are having such trouble with Palin is that she's never listened to radical leftists telling her that nasty, nasty men put a glass ceiling in her way, so rather than, say, becoming America's first female Vice-President, she should be bitching about how transgender' perverts have been unfairly left out of the Civil Rights Act over two-for-one margaritas at TGI Fridays. Simply put: she doesn't need you.

I worry for my daughter, growing up in a country where wailing socialist harpies like Feministing's castratrix-in-chief Jessica Valenti can get a pat on the head for writing potty-mouthed screeds like 'Full Frontal Feminism' while a true role model like Gov. Palin is subjected to every slander her 'sisters' can think up.

That's some good solidarity there girls.

Posted by Locke September 17 2008

Comments (14)

Greetings from Soviet America

Apparently Capitalism isn't good enough any more, so the Federal Government is buying AIG.

Quote:

In a move aimed at averting a new global economic shock, the US Federal Reserve agreed an unprecedented 85-billion-dollar rescue loan for American International Group. The deal, sealed late Tuesday, saved AIG from collapse and gave the US government a 79.9 percent stake in the insurance behemoth.

Say, since we've decided to abandon our principles because a few clans of immigrants can't get credit on Beverley Hills super-mansions why not snap up that tasty looking healthcare system? It works in Europe, right Michael Moore? (Wrong)
It looks like Khrushchev was right: they're burying us as we speak.

Posted by Locke September 17 2008

Comments (16)

David Foster Wallace

I don't normally do requests, but something about RobertCQuin@missiongossip.com's e-mail struck me as a little odd:

> Hi Locke – love the site, very witty! Just wondering if you've heard the news about the tragic death of David Foster Wallace – one of the most important American writers??? What's your take on the author and his work???

Why have I not heard of 'one of the most important American writers'? Having been an American for the last thirty-one years I would have surely come across a novelist and essayist whose suicide got every trendy Liberal website from Salon to Villagevoice to write something other than another two-thousand word reach-around to Hussein-Obama.

Conservapedia has this on him:

David Foster Wallace (February 21, 1962 – September 12, 2008) was a professor at Pomona College in Claremont, California, and a writer of both fiction and nonfiction. He is perhaps best known for his 1996 novel Infinite Jest, which was named by Time Magazine as one of the 100 best English-language novels from 1923 to 2005.

Born in Ithaca, New York, Wallace was a tennis player and majored in English and philosophy. Aside from writing novels, he wrote short stories in magazines such as **Playboy**, **The Paris Review, The New Yorker** and others. Wallace has written some nonfiction. He covered Senator John McCain's 2000 Presidential campaign and the September 11, 2001 attacks for Rolling Stone. **A liberal, he has been a critic of the United States and War on Terrorism. In the November 2007 issue of The Atlantic, he said 'Have we become so selfish and scared that we don't even want to consider whether some things trump safety?'** (Emphasis mine)

Wallace committed suicide by hanging on Friday, September 12, 2008 at age 46 because of depression.

The Conservapedia article is barely a stub for a good reason: David Foster Wallace has nothing of any interest to say to anyone who doesn't share his liberal extremist views. Even if he did I doubt anybody not stoned out of their minds in the Berkeley dorms would be able to understand it. When braving the Darwinist cesspool Wikipedia for further details I found out not just what he writes (terrorist apologia) but how:

'Wallace's novels often meld writing in various modes or voices, and incorporate jargon and vocabulary (sometimes invented) from a wide variety of fields. He liked to use obscure words and had a self-proclaimed love affair with the *Oxford English Dictionary*. His prose style features many unusual stylistic devices, from self-generated abbreviations and acronyms to long sentences with many clauses.'

Gareth Watkins

Sounds like garbage, reads like garbage, but don't let that fool you, it really is garbage.

It wouldn't be Christian of me to take any joy in one of God's children taking his own life after years of depression, even if it does mean one less person hating America, but I will say this: Wallace's life illustrates the dangers of liberalism. Hating the country you were born in, refusing to believe in the God who made you and burying your head in books are not elements of a happy or productive life. Liberalism is to educated whites what gang culture is to colored communities, leading millions of otherwise happy and productive Americans into drugs and suicide.

The highlighted section above sums up the horrible irony of his life quite succinctly: **'Have we become so selfish and scared that we don't even want to consider whether some things trump safety?'** If you turn the question around and ask it of Wallace then you have to answer that yes, he believed that something – his sadness and pain – trumped not only his own life but everything. Tellingly, Wallace didn't have children. If he did then he would have known that nothing trumps safety.

In happier news, I've found a church for Danyelle's Baptism. The good people of Columbus United Methodist Church will be doing the honors. I'm pleased to announce that Alfred Erickson, a close friend from Yale whose support of the Republican party and America in general has been a constant inspiration to me, and his lovely wife Martha have agreed to be little Danyelle's godparents.

Posted by Locke September 16 2008

Comments (45)

Clarification

After everything that's happened I still maintain that we in the United States of America have the best healthcare system in the world. Bar none.

Posted by Locke September 12 2008

Comments (82)

Growing up under Hussein-Obama

I'm sorry that I haven't wrote in a while. It's inexcusable. We are at a vital point in our nation's history, politically and economically, and there *must* be voices dissenting against the liberal consensus. There *must*.

Those of you that have been with this site a while know that I believe in plain speaking, so here it goes: I do not believe that McCain and Palin can win this election.

I believe that they deserve it, that they are the right choice for the nation and that they've run a decent, honest campaign. But this is not enough.
The idea of 'The First Black President' is too tempting for a nation used to grazing on Jon Stewart, NPR, the New York Times and a defeatist Hollywood. He's that black friend that every latte-guzzler has, but can't name. He's a no effort, no maintenance, fast-food panacea for an invented disease: America's 'race problem'. This idea is so widespread, its propagandists so slick and persuasive, that we'll put somebody with known ties to terrorism into the White House.

I'll grit my teeth and bear it – I've already suffered through a 'black president' during the Clinton years. My daughter, on the other hand, is going to grow up in his schools, with his values in every media outlet (mark my words – the 'Fairness Doctrine' will come back with a vengeance). Sooner or later we'll put his face on the dollar bill – somebody will mention that Washington owned slaves and that will be that. I'll do my best to raise her with American, Christian and, yes, White values, always knowing that it won't be enough.
Take a look at the abstinence movement, for example. There you have good people doing a good thing for the nation's youth, with truth, scripture and the Federal government on their side. Yet it doesn't make

Gareth Watkins

a difference – abstinence-only sex-ed doesn't delay young people giving up their bodies for one second. How can it when Hollywood is pushing its activist agenda on every film screen and television set?

Now, with a Hussein-Obama victory almost certain, socialists the nation over will be coming out of the Humanities department and into positions of power. They'll come with the conviction that history has proved them right when their new best buddy orders American troops to retreat from Iraq and the economy collapses around our ears. Don't imagine for a second that they're not interested in indoctrinating our children, that making them every bit as Godless, strung-out and hopeless as they are isn't part of their plan. How long before they decide that certain people aren't fit to raise a child in happy-rainbow America?

Not long.

Posted by Locke September 12 2008

Comments (18)

(untitled post)

I don't owe you anything. This is a blog about POLITICS. You know nothing about me save what I write here. I don't need your voyeurism disguised as 'support'. I am sick of your need to know every. Damn. Detail. Worse than the rubber-neckers are the fucking simpering hippies who want – no need me to 'grow' and 'change' to validate their sissy worldview.

Why can't I not need anything? Why is that not allowed? Why is pain not OK?

What happened to me HAPPENED TO ME – you can't have it.

Posted by Locke August 28 2008

Comments (102)

(untitled post)

My wife is dead. The baby is a girl.

Posted by Locke August 20 2008

Comments (386)

Gareth Watkins has studied creative writing and literature in the US and UK. After graduating from UEA he will be finishing his first novel.

Kristian White

He Sells Hairstyles

My next client is waiting. I catch a flicker of knickers in the mirror. I've left the gown off until after I shampoo her. I tell her it's because it's hot. I say it's great weather we're having. But that's not it. That's not it at all. It's because she's hot and I'm bored.
    My gaze drops – she catches me. I offer her coffee – she wants tea. I grab a trainee. I tell her to fetch it.
    She frowns – I smile – she sparkles – I flash, a row of white caps.
    I say –
    What can I do for you?
    She says –
    I'd like a change.
    What sort of change?
    I want to look different.
    I slap down glossy mags and cutting collections. She licks a finger and flicks the pages. There are pictures of pop idols and rock idols, teen idols and screen idols, It girls and tit girls, sports stars in fast cars and Czech babes in Wonderbras.
    She shrugs, lips purse, she says – I've had long hair for ages. I've had it for longer than I can remember. I'm a bit nervous.
    She pauses. I tick over.
    She asks me –
    What would you do if you had your way?
    She has long, thick, straight hair. It is perfect – wild – un-styled, untainted, un-tinted. Un-manipulated – the world in my hands. But I

hold back. Clients think they've made your day when they offer themselves up as a blank canvas. But they haven't. It just means you waste time trying to read their minds then rush to finish the job in time. There's always a dream. Dig in. You'll find it in the bottom of her handbag or fluff deep in a coat pocket – a magazine cut-out shyly folded, a snapshot of love, a secret hope.

And I was hoping. I was hoping for something easy. I was hoping for a quick fix. A bread and butter cut. In and out, job done and time left to knock back black coffee. But no. There's no such thing as a blank canvas. Everything has a colour.

So I look at her and I measure her – her eyes, her jawline, her head shape. She could suit anything. Any cut you could think of. So I say –

Let's cut it short.

Short?

Short.

How short?

Short so you have a real change.

How short is that?

Sixties short. Think revolution – the Sexual revolution. Think Twiggy, Jean Shrimpton, Mary Quant. Think Isadora Duncan.

Isadora who?

Exactly. Now think evolution – evolution revolution. Think edginess, impact – think fashion explosion. Think the Style ABC.

The Style ABC?

Aniston – Beckham – Kylie.

Kylie? But –

Yeah. I know. I don't get that either. Anyway, stick them all in a blender, add a Spice Girl or two, a sprinkle of Hilton, a pinch of Winehouse, salt to taste – et VOILA. The cut of today. A classic with a modern twist. Sassoon meets Stafford.

Stafford?

Lee Stafford.

The one with the dog?

The silver dog on a pink pot.

I know the one. It's sold in most shops.

That's right. But enough of names and fame. How about you? Are you

game or what?
Game for what?
A short cut.
Have you got a picture?
I smile. I shut my eyes. I scream soundlessly. The mirror shivers, shakes, cracks – rains, cuts and maims – the salon floor runs red. And I think – I want my rights. I want a gun. I say no to slow-killing cancer. I want the fundamental right to a quick death. I plead – Legalise suicide. I say –

There is no picture. This is an original. Don't you want to be original? Don't you want to be the first? Winners write history – losers get lost.
She laughs – she nods – she smirks.
She looks at me like she's trying to suss me – she's toying with consent but she doesn't quite trust me. And why should she? She doesn't know me. She's never seen me. And what's so special about spontaneity anyway? It's so old hat. These days it's all about assurances. Contracts count. Signatures are sexy. If your name's not in print you don't exist. No one leaves the future to chance. Not anymore. Instinct died of AIDS.

We are locked. But I must make a move. The receptionist is giving me that look. It's her job. She does the bookings. She splits the day into appointments – scribbled names in blocks in columns – then makes sure we stick to them. If she doesn't keep time inside the blocks the column will crumble and the salon will fall.

I say –
So what do you say?
She says –
Does it have to be so short? Couldn't you cut something inbetween?
I hate those words. I hear them all the time. Inbetween. There is no inbetween – no compromise – no concurrence of the grey and wise. We are reflections in each other's eyes. I say –

I could cut something inbetween but it wouldn't be much of a change. It would still be the same old you.

And it's true. I could cut something inbetween. Of course I could. It's just a technicality. But it wouldn't hang right. It'd be like Michelangelo's David with a big dick.

She pauses. She ponders. She says –

And you think short will definitely suit me?
I'd stake my country cottage on it.
You have a cottage?
Not yet.
She is confused.
    I messed up. Rule number one – Never corner a client. And with all my charm and all my training – still – I did just that. I hit her with too much jargon in a short space. She can't picture what's on my mind – I can't picture what's on hers. And that's why – in this land of wax and spray – consultation is king. Happy clients are career makers and blind ideals will empty chairs of broken hearts that won't be healed. And I should know. I've had so many clients that on some days I don't remember who or what I was before – like my life just quietly fell away behind me word by word. And alone in the dark I ask myself how with all the good intentions in the world I still screw up again and again? And I think – it's time. That's all it is. Just time. Give a man a million years and he'd be Jesus. But there is never enough time. I could never be perfect. I'm not even sure if I'm good. But I am fast.
    She frowns – she looks around. She looks forward – she looks down at her hands. Her nails are orange. They are false. I can spot the subtle joins. I see enough every day to spot a fake. My gaze traces the line of her fingers. I follow their movements. She has long fingers – fluid fingers. I want her to encircle me with them. I wonder how many men she's ringed.
    She looks up and I hide the thought.
    She squints. I squirm. She smiles.
    She says –
Let's do it.
    I seat her in the basin chair and tilt her head back. I stand behind. It's the perfect angle to ogle and I do. My breathing soon tunes to the rise and fall of her cup, accompanied by the static of gossip and dryers.
    I shampoo.
    I press my fingers into her roots and rub. I begin with small circular motions then expand kaleidoscopically.
    I rinse.
    The water drains.

I slap on a dollop of Smokey Oak and Honey treatment conditioner. This will give a deep shine to the finish.

I pat flat the paste and work it in – from roots to ends – then comb it through using a wide tooth black comb.

She says –

That smells gorgeous. It smells like you could eat it.

She laughs. I laugh but I don't think it's funny. Not any more. It was funny the first few times. Everything was funny in the beginning. Everything was fun. There were hairstyles to learn and hairstyles to invent. Now it feels like I've done them all over and over. There are only so many combinations to try. Everyone always asks me what's in fashion. They ask me – what's the latest hairstyle? I recite the latest Vogue but inside I think – It's only clones and clones of clones. That's what it is.

Next I apply a Shiatsu head massage.

She closes her eyes. Her breathing deepens. Her lips part. I inhale her sweetness. I bathe in her light.

I rinse her – slick back – with cool water. She opens her eyes. Then she says it.

She says –

Have you ever seen a star in daytime?

What?

A star in daytime?

I stare at her like a lunatic.

I didn't think you could but I saw one today.

Despite the rush I can't help thinking about it. Because I can't remember the last time I actually looked up at the sky never mind the stars.

I gown her up.

I section off a centre parting and clip it tight.
I comb down a section.
I am exact – I am calculation – I am precision.

I unsheathe my scissors.
I watch her in the mirror – red-faced and worried. She looks like she's agreed to have sex with me and changed her mind and what's more I'm blocking the bedroom door.

The music stops.
Everything is still. Everyone is motionless. Everything is –

Scissors snap shut.
Wet locks drop to the floor next to her jaw. Her neck is nude pink as painted whores on coffee shop walls.

I take another and another – small sections between my fingers – and snip and snip.
I follow the guideline.
I check the balance.

I am balance.

She says – How's it looking? She can see how it's looking but no one trusts their own reflection.

I angle.
I over-direct.
I cross-check.

I am precision.

I say – This is going to look amazing. You're lucky. Not everyone can carry this off. But with your bone structure and eye colour it's a cinch.
Really?
Yes. You look like that actress. That French one. Oh, what's her name? She's in that film.
Amélie?
Who? Oh yes – that's her.
She beams. I've stroked her vanity G spot and she opens up wide to

me. But I don't rush in. Not yet. I watch her watch me in the mirror and I see in her eyes a me I can never be but for a moment – framed in glass – I can almost believe in –
   A perfect me.

   I blow dry
   I free-hand – I slice.
   I back-cut – I twist cut – I style.

   I am clarity. I am vision.

   I finish. I help her up and hold the gown. She shrugs it off. She slides back into her summer denim and pays by debit card. She buys each exciting product they place in her hands – each overpriced product I told her to buy not because she needed it but because I had to. Because all the talent in the world will only buy you an unmarked grave if you don't sell.
   I open the door for her.
   She smiles – she hugs me – she tips me.
   She walks off.
   I hold out my arm. She shrinks to a dot. It hurts. It always does. But I heal quick. By the time my next one arrives she'll be forgotten – just a name in a block in a book.
   My eyes rise to the blue blue sky past the glassy sun to forever. For a moment I think I see a star. Then it's gone.

Kristian is currently finishing a novel named *He Sells Hairstyles* before embarking on a novel about the UK surfing scene called *The Endless Bummer*.

Nisha Woolfstein

Other Girls
An extract from a novel

Mr Gander leans back against the fading brocade of the armchair. Light snags softly against his face, like the finest of nets. It catches so slightly on the corners of the room, on the leaves of entwining plants that today all pale to a faint green. The outside appears to glow through the transparent leaves, and the cluttered furniture, which looks as if it grew out of the room hundreds of years ago, is almost indistinguishable from the plants in the sunlight. Above a neglected fireplace, the mantelpiece had been refined long ago into an altar of sorts. Gilt candlesticks reflect, and the light fractures and multiplies in the cut-glass mirror above.

'They don't understand you see, Sweetheart.' Lifting his hand slowly towards the window, he brushes dust particles from the arm of his chair which flair minutely in the filtered sunlight. 'They're blind. The world out there, all blind ...'

Marta thinks of Mary Poppins, of the dad who didn't see the bird woman. *Feed the birds, tuppence a bag ...*

'They don't see what's in front of their noses,' she says.

'They don't like me to tell them otherwise.'

She shakes her head, then thinks maybe it would be better to nod.

'They think "two plus two" ... They don't think. They never think,' he says.

'They want it simple.'

'Why four? Will they believe me, Sweetheart? I try to tell them, *five*, think. Five!'

'They're all scared.'
'What's two plus two?'
'Five.'
'You see,' he says. 'Possibility. It can make five. You see.'
Marta touches the pendant on the light silver chain around her neck and leans her head onto her arm. The pendant is a tiny square of silver containing a portrait of the Virgin Mary, her profile smaller than a child's fingernail. The Virgin is depicted in relief, as if, in the curve of her cheek, her head, and her shoulder, she is trying to push her way through the metal. Marta hasn't taken the necklace off for three years. Mr Gander had given her the pendant for her ninth birthday in a little gold box. She had thought it was gold, but actually the metal is brass, its lid inlaid with tessellated fragments of mother-of-pearl.

'The world was supposed to be joyful. That's why He came back! Did anyone listen, out there?' He nods towards the window.

'I don't think so, no.' Marta looks at him and then back at the window, its hazy bright outlines.

'How can anyone be happy out there! How can you? Impossible. Remember what happened to the Master.'

Marta thinks of Mary's face, quite sad and empty looking. She looks up to the little statuettes on the makeshift altar: Jesus and Mary, like the ones in a church. 'You are the only one', he has often said. The only one that can make it all right.

'They crucified him,' she said.

'Yes. You see! That's why, this time, it must all be behind closed doors, Sweetheart. Behind closed doors.'

Marta looks towards the door, past the cabinet of unknown books. What were they about? Once she had asked him if she could look at them. He had opened the cabinet right away. She had sat on the floor by his chair taking them down from the shelf. They were old books with no pictures, and no stories. One was called 'Almanac'; another was a list of kings. There was just one which had a kind of story, about Egypt. She wondered now what the story might be like. Mr Gander's eyes are not quite closed.

'Could I borrow one of your books?' She whispers it, not wanting to wake him.

He nods with half a start, but his head sinks again, his neck condensing. Marta moves quietly and lifts the book from the cabinet. In the milk-yellow light Mr Gander's head has dropped. His basking chin touches the collar of his waistcoat. He is almost asleep, his feet flat on the floor, in sandy-coloured slippers. She decides it is a good time to slip out of the room.

From the cold, sparse bathroom across the narrow hallway, sounds flutter through the small open window like dazed insects. Calling neighbours, laughter and shouts of children, and the birds; 'my my, my my' a chaffinch sings. The toilet seat is so cold that she shudders. Tiles are printed with a pattern of green snowflakes. The bath stands on flat feet, as if it is ready to run, but has forgotten how. There is a basin, soap – hard as a skinny cuttlefish – a thin beige hand towel. Mr Gander's toilet paper. Why does he buy it? She has sometimes thought of asking him, but it just seems too rude a question. It is the crackly kind that filled the regimented rows of the toilet cubicles at school. But this is scratchier, colder and thinner still, like neatly cut autumn leaves dipped in wax.

He looks around brightly as she comes back into the living room.

'Ah, Sweetheart! There you are. I thought you had gone and left me.' He smiles towards her and she stands a second by the door and laughs quietly, feeling somehow flattered.

'Would I?' She smiles back at him. 'Of course I wouldn't leave you!'

Mr Gander pats the arm of his chair and, still seated, drags at a little hardback chair beside the cabinet. Marta takes it, pulling the chair right next to his armchair.

'Ah, that's better.' He takes her hand and plants a long kiss upon the small back of her hand, at the edge of her wrist. He keeps the hand in his lap, holding it like something long lost. 'Do y'promise you'll never leave me?' He looks at her without laughing.

Marta, sitting on the wooden chair, finds herself looking directly into Mr Gander's face. She almost has to look down to meet his eyes. He looks serious, holding her hand tightly, stroking it ever so slightly.

'Of course I'll never leave you.'

Mr Gander raises his eyebrows, and Marta glances towards the altar, then towards the window, in quiet panic. She looks back to Mr Gander's face. His eyes are questioning, almost accusing, as if reading her mind.

Nisha Woolfstein

'I'll always be here,' she says, 'with you, with them. You know I will.'

The edges of a smile inch around his lips. A group of children shout and laugh as they ride by on BMXs; as if the window was a television and the children a programme, switched on, and then off again.

'It's a dark place, out there.' He lets go of her hand and gestures towards the quiet street.

Marta sees cool sunshine on the grass verges. She fidgets and sits on her hands.

'It is, it is,' he continues. 'And the light must overcome the dark, eventually. It must.'

Marta looks again at the sunshine through the window. 'Shall we go outside?'

'You want to go into the garden?' He looks at her as if on the edge of sleep again.

'We could.'

'Not yet,' he says. His eyes close.

The squat sofa weighs down as Marta unloads homework from her school bag. The story about Egypt had been quick to read, but it had worried her.

'My goodness.' Mr Gander sighs, waking to the rustling of papers.

Marta feels lumbering, as if she were growing perceptibly by the second, overtaking even the fertility of the plants.

'Well,' she stutters, unusually self-conscious, as if Mr Gander was aware of her growing proportions.

'What's all that for then, eh?' He gestures to the papers and folders which cascade across the sofa.

Marta continues rearranging and laughs awkwardly. 'Good question.' She takes off her jumper and attempts to smooth down a static school shirt. 'I was thinking about Egypt.'

'Egypt, yes, what about it?'

'Something I just read, in this story.'

The book is nondescript, with covers like slate. He has forgotten about it. Mr Gander's attention drifts, his eyes fixed upon the middle distance.

'I see, what is it then? What?'

Marta wanders towards the window. As she looks back from behind the solid table, the new view of such a familiar room is strange. Everything in the room seems to be cut into fine panels of the palest silvery light – where had it come from? She turns to the window and the street displays an afternoon the colour of army uniforms; it does not explain such a fine, pale light. Egypt, she thinks.

'They sacrificed an enormous white bull.'

He nods as if to say, yes, of course, that happens all the time.

'A beautiful bull. It said it was the biggest in the city, in the book.'

'Yes.'

'Instead of properly killing it, they cut off its, you know, down there.'

'I see.'

His face is simple, blank like a boy's. Marta waits. But he looks at her intently. Maybe he's not pleased that she borrowed the book. Corners of light flit around the room like dragonflies' wings.

'Sometimes you remind me of another girl who used to come and visit me.'

'Here?' She is surprised. 'Another girl?' The pale light seems to pause as he nods.

'Years back now. In Lamington Road.'

Why does Marta picture a tent out of doors? A tent where a girl just like herself visits Mr Gander. In the tent, Mr Gander is a young man.

'One day she never came back. Just like that.'

'What happened to her?' An empty tent, Marta thinks.

He shrugs with exaggerated hands outstretched. 'I heard her family moved away, but that was later.'

Is it only surprise Marta feels, or something else? As if the other girl has just taken something from her. She sits back down. She couldn't say what it is that has been taken. He looks at her directly, urgently, ready to speak, almost imploring, as if he were no older than her.

'Before that. When I was sixteen, Sweetheart. I loved a girl.'

She feels a shudder of cold reality as if the girl were with them here.

'Lovely, she was.'

A flickering ghost sits next to her on the sofa.

'I didn't understand. They stopped it you see.'

'Why? Stopped what?'

Nisha Woolfstein

'I don't know. What had I done?'

She answers him slowly. 'I don't know, nothing, what did you do?' Another girl? Two others? Bits of her feel frostbitten. Her hands look pale.

'Nothing, Sweetheart! I wouldn't have done!' He brings his hand down slap upon the slippery arm of his chair. The movement looks as if it should continue, like a ski jump, but he stops still as a stone.

'That's why it was so awful.'

'Awful?' She nods for him to continue.

'She was twelve, same as you. Oh I loved her, Sweetheart.'

'What happened?'

'Daisy. She had lightish hair, lighter than yours. Lived some streets away. Months, just for months. But we were always together.'

'That's all right, isn't it?'

'Her family found out. They were furious. Mine too, my mother. They said, her family, they said, "That's it". I wasn't to go near her. Couldn't even go into her street again.'

'Why?'

'I don't know. I had done nothing. Nothing!' He rests his elbow on the branching arms of the chair, his palms against the sharp ridge of his cheeks, and looks away from her, towards the forested corners of the room.

'Terribly, I loved her terribly.'

Marta looks towards the wallpaper, the red of the Chinese fishermen, their little nets frozen against the walls, and she just thinks about how that girl had been lucky. The story seems beautiful, tragic like a book or a film, but real. The wallpaper with its fishermen and miniature pagodas stays still now. How much easier it must be if the boy is sixteen, and you can whisper about them to your friends. Maybe the girl cried with her friends afterwards. Marta glances at the pile of papers which rests against her. They seem to crumble, to fade away in the pale brittle light. They seem stupid, a stupid pile of homework. No help at all.

Nisha Woolfstein grew up in England and has lived and worked in Spain, India and the US. Her short fiction has appeared in the *Late Night River Lights* anthology of new writing. She graduated from Cambridge in 2007 and is currently working on her first novel, about a small twentieth-century cult.

Life Writing

Introduction by **Kathryn Hughes**

Philippa Stewart

Life has never seemed quite so topsy-turvy as it does right now. As this anthology goes to press, politicians of all stripes are queuing up to give a plausible account of themselves and what might politely be called their lifestyle choices. Second homes, moats, manure and KitKats are all being set before sceptical taxpayers as vital items without which no public servant can perform their proper duties. It is like being given permission to rifle through other people's drawers and pronounce on what you find.

All of which creates a buoyant atmosphere for the MA in Life Writing to flourish. Of course, studying the history and practice of biography involves a lot more than simply snooping on someone's expense claims. Still, a healthy curiosity in the petty details of some of history's most intriguing lives is as good a place as any to start. On top of that you've got to add a firm grasp of the main political and social narratives of the time, a rat-like cunning for tracking down new sources, a novelist's eye for character, a dramatist's skill at plot and a flair for language that wouldn't shame a poet. Mix all those together, and you might just have the ingredients for a good biography.

This year's Life Writing contribution from Philippa Stewart demonstrates all these qualities, and more. She has set herself the task of tracking down the early family life of Elizabeth Garrett Anderson and Millicent Fawcett, those extraordinary Suffolk sisters who did so much to transform the possibilities and opportunities available to other Victorian women. Elizabeth was Britain's first female doctor while Millicent was a tireless campaigner for female suffrage. Glorious though their journeys may have been, Stewart has uncovered a fascinating story of early origins which begins in a small room over a pawnbroker's shop in Whitechapel. Exactly the sort of accommodation which our currently chastened MPs might, with hindsight, have been wiser to have chosen.

KH

Philippa Stewart

A Family of Firsts: The Garretts of Aldeburgh

Introduction

In October 2008 the Royal Mail issued a collection of special stamps celebrating Women of Distinction. Surprisingly, although they featured only six women, two of them were sisters. They were Elizabeth Garrett Anderson (1836–1917), the first woman in England to qualify as a doctor and also the country's first woman mayor, and Millicent Garrett Fawcett (1847–1929), co-founder of Newnham College, Cambridge, and a tireless campaigner for women's rights, who played a major role in securing the vote for women.

Equally surprising is that these two sisters were not metropolitan sophisticates, nor raised in a household with a tradition of intellectual or radical fervour. Instead they grew up in a sleepy corner of Suffolk, on the coast at Aldeburgh; in the mid-nineteenth century this was a slightly neglected town whose main source of revenue, fishing, was in decline. The girls' father was a merchant, their mother an innkeeper's daughter. Yet among the family's ten children were other outstanding pioneers: a daughter who started a home decorating business and was the first woman to write a book on interior design; a son who became President of the Law Society and was the first lawyer to accept women pupils in his chambers.

What was it about this family that produced such an efflorescence of talent, enterprise and courage? What combination of genes and upbringing enabled them to break the social mould and achieve so much? In my attempt to find answers to these questions, I set out to explore the family's background and how the children were raised.

Chapter One – London Beginnings

If you walk along Crawford Street in Marylebone, central London, you will find the Beehive public house on the south side of the street, on the corner of Montagu Mews. It claims to be one of London's oldest inns and today is a thriving gastro-pub, with tables for eating outside and laughing crowds in the well-lit interior.

Nearly 200 years ago, in the 1820s and '30s, the Beehive was equally prosperous. Its landlord in those days was the enterprising John Dunnell, a Suffolk man from the 'lost city' of Dunwich (in the early Middle Ages Dunwich had been one of the most important settlements on the east coast, but by the sixteenth century much of the town had been lost to the sea; according to local legend you can still hear the bells from its sunken churches chiming under the waves). As well as the Beehive, John Dunnell owned at least two more pubs in London, and several other businesses including a pawnbroker's shop in the East End and a jeweller's near Covent Garden. He had married a Dunwich girl, Elizabeth Gayford, in about 1805 and they set up home in London, first in City Road near the Angel and later in Acacia Road, St John's Wood. They had ten children: three sons and seven daughters.

Despite living in London the Dunnells maintained strong links with Suffolk. In October 1828 their eldest daughter, Elizabeth, married Richard Garrett from Leiston, a small town a few miles south of Dunwich. John Dunnell and his wife must have been delighted with the match. As the eldest son, Richard Garrett was in line to inherit his family's business manufacturing agricultural machines; at the age of 19, two years before his marriage, he had already been appointed Financial Director of the Garrett Works in Leiston, and clearly had excellent prospects. (Indeed, a few years later, his father retired early to become a farmer and Richard Garrett successfully took over as Managing Director of the works.)

Given this happy relationship between the two families, it was quite natural that John Dunnell should have extended a warm welcome to

Philippa Stewart

Richard Garrett's youngest brother, Newson – who in the autumn of 1830, in the traditional manner of many younger sons, had travelled to London to make his fortune. London at the time was abuzz with new beginnings: there was a new king, William IV, on the throne; an elderly Duke of Wellington was about to be ousted as Prime Minister by the reforming Lord Grey; and everyone was talking about a new mode of transport, the railway. The world's first passenger-carrying line, the Liverpool and Manchester Railway, opened on 15th September of that year – a day only slightly marred by the death of the MP for Liverpool, William Huskisson, who was hit by Stephenson's engine, Rocket. With all these changes in the air, London was full of rumour, gossip and discussion; it must have seemed an exciting place to the tall, fair-haired 18 year old, fresh from the wide skies and peaceful meadows of east Suffolk.

Newson Garrett settled in Islington but soon was a regular visitor to the Beehive and to the Dunnell home in Acacia Road. In due course, following the example set by his brother, Newson fell in love with the third of the Dunnell daughters, Louisa, and she with him. Having obtained her father's permission (Louisa was not yet 21), they were married in the imposing church of St Mary's in Bryanston Square, just a few minutes down the road from the Beehive, on 5th April 1834.

So what were they like, this young couple with their shared Suffolk roots, starting life together in London? All the descriptions of Newson Garrett concur in mentioning his tremendous energy and his combativeness. He was a good-looking man, above average in height, with a mop of blond hair and piercing blue eyes. A neighbour who had known him when he was young said he was 'the most beautiful child she had ever seen'. Newson had attended school at Grundisburgh, near Woodbridge in Suffolk, so was better educated than many of his contemporaries, but he was probably too impatient to be a good student. All his life jokes were made about his handwriting; this may explain why, on his wedding day, he allowed his bride to sign his name in the marriage register, simply acknowledging it by a cross alongside. But Newson was shrewd, full of ambitious plans, and fiercely protective of his own.

His young wife Louisa was not especially good-looking; later portraits show her with a slightly pinched face and dark hair pulled into a tight bun. But she was kind and intelligent, and an excellent household manager; more crucially, perhaps, she was fired by a deep religious conviction inherited from her mother, and this gave her tremendous determination and strength of character. Together she and Newson made a formidable team.

John Dunnell was sufficiently impressed by the energy and self-confidence of his new son-in-law to appoint Newson as manager of the pawnbroking business he owned at No. 1 Commercial Road, Whitechapel, in the East End of London. As an added benefit there was a flat above the shop where Newson and Louisa could live.

Whitechapel in the 1830s had not yet seen the two great waves of immigration, Irish and Jewish, that would transform it in the second half of the nineteenth century – but it was already under pressure as factories and industry spread eastwards along the banks of the River Thames. Commercial Road was one of the main thoroughfares from the West India Docks where sugar cane from the Caribbean was unloaded. From there the sugar was carried in horse-drawn carts to be processed in one of the many 'sugar bakeries' that had been built in Whitechapel. The rumble of heavy carts laden with sugar cane continued day and night; the air was thick with sickly sweet fumes, and sulphurous smoke blackened streets and houses. The whole area was noisy, dirty and crowded, and without any open spaces where children could play. It was not the ideal place for a young couple to set up home.

The Garretts' first child Louisa (usually called 'Louie' to avoid confusion with her mother) was born in February 1835. Another daughter, Elizabeth, followed soon after in June 1836, and then in November 1837 came the longed-for son, proudly christened Dunnell Newson to represent the link between the two families. The little boy survived the winter but died the following May. Louisa Garrett was prostrate with grief. For the rest of her life she never forgot the son she had lost and used to tell her younger children how, when he had died, 'she had kneeled down and prayed God to take her too'.

During the summer of 1838, perhaps in an attempt to cheer up his wife, Newson Garrett commissioned a painting of the family – an unusual thing to do for a man of his relatively lowly status. The painting itself has since been lost but a photograph of it remains, showing the proud parents with their daughters aged two and three. Newson Garrett wears a frock-coat, Louisa a sprigged dress cut low off the shoulder, while the two children look plump and happy. It is a charming picture of a young family smiling bravely at the world.

The death of baby Dunnell must have spurred the family to move. Certainly, by the end of 1838, they had left Commercial Road and were installed at 142 Long Acre, round the corner from St Martin's Lane. Here Newson Garrett became manager of another of his father-in-law's pawnbroking businesses, this time a rather grander shop which combined a pawnbroker's with selling jewellery. The area, too, was much more pleasant. Instead of grimy sugar carts they could watch carts up from the country laden with fruit and vegetables, making their way to the market at nearby Covent Garden. The trees and green expanse of St James's Park were within easy walking distance. And, for the children, there were plenty of stables and horses to visit, and fine coachmen from the Royal Mews to admire.

In later years Elizabeth Garrett Anderson used to recall how she had been woken one night and lifted onto her father's shoulder, to watch the Queen and Prince Albert in 'a fairytale scene of gilded coaches', making their way through cheering crowds to the opera at Covent Garden. Her mother had fretted about the four-year-old Elizabeth being up so late but her father was adamant, saying: 'Of course the child must see it; she will remember it all her life.' And she did.

In June 1839, a second son was born and christened Newson Dunnell; another boy, Edmund, came in November 1840. By now, with a growing family to support and with his brother Richard already making a notable success of running the Garrett Works in Leiston, Newson Garrett must have felt that the time had come for him to strike out on his own. His father had died in 1837, leaving most of his money tied up in the works that Richard had inherited. But Newson had received a quarter share of the 'stock, implements and interests on hand', to be paid in instalments; he had accumulated some savings, and Louisa also had a little money of her own. Naturally enough, their thoughts turned to their home county of Suffolk.

On 2nd August 1840 Newson was staying with his brother in Leiston when he wrote excitedly to Louisa still in London: 'Mr Fennell of Aldboro' is very ill and his business is to be disposed of. Our dear brother [Richard] here thinks very highly of it and in the liberality of his heart ... has offered to do anything in his power if we should like to have it ... He flatters me by saying that he is sure I could manage it, and that it is a very profitable concern.' On 18th August Newson wrote again with details of the financial arrangements, asking Louisa to share them with her father, and mentioned a house in Aldeburgh that he was negotiating to buy.

With some help from John Dunnell the deal was done. Newson Garrett became the owner of Mr Fennell's corn and coal warehouse at Snape Bridge, a few miles inland up the River Alde, and of The Uplands, a square Georgian house opposite the parish church of St Peter and St Paul, on the hill above Aldeburgh.

In March 1841, as the storms of winter began to ease, the family finally embarked on their sea journey back to Suffolk. Newson Garrett was then 29, his wife a year younger, and they already had four children of whom the eldest had just turned six. With courage and determination they set sail for a new life.

Chapter Two – An Aldeburgh Childhood

Chapter Three – School Days and Friends

Chapter Four – Ma and Pa

Chapter Five – Out into the World

Conclusion

Philippa Stewart worked in publishing for some 35 years, specialising in children's books and particularly children's non-fiction. Now retired from corporate life and living in Suffolk, she is pursuing her interest in writing by researching the achievements of a local Suffolk family, the Garretts.

UEA Creative Writing Anthology 2009

Scriptwriting

Introduction by **Val Taylor**

Drew Castalia
Ben Craib
Chris Duffill
Jake Marcet

Ruth Selwyn-Crome
William Simpson
Andrew Strike
Sunitha Webster

It seems counter-intuitive, in a creative writing course, for tutors to urge students to write less. Scriptwriting, however, is a very lean form of writing. On the page, excess is immediately visible to the experienced eye: there is too much ink, too little white space. Excess is also audible, for in workshops we read scripts aloud. It's apparent when a character has said what she has to say and should stop; when a look or gesture would say it better; or when a stage (or scene) direction has too many frills and flourishes.

Excess, though, is not synonymous with redundancy. There is necessary 'fat'. If this is cut, the script loses energy, warmth and, sometimes, depth. Unnecessary 'fat' weighs the script down; cut it, and fluency re-appears. The script is lighter, defter. Bouncier. UEA scriptwriters must learn to distinguish between muscle and fat, and be ready to free the script from – at times – some of their favourite lines.

Scripts can also be under-nourished. Sometimes there is too little on the page: not enough detail, the wrong detail. Or a character doesn't say, do or imply enough to let him grab the story and run. It can be harder to correct than excess; adding is less successful than cutting. A 'thin' scene must be re-imagined from scratch, not padded: the muscle of a scene should be grown, not painted on.

Scriptwriters must give us so much but no more. How much, is a question of judgment, informed by their individual style, and intellectual and emotional investment in the story. Whilst being fully immersed in each scripted moment, they must also stand apart, weighing the moment. They must be in two places at once.

It's quite a trick.

VT

Drew Castalia

The Last Explorer

EXT. FREEZING QUAY – KING'S LYNN – DAY

A thick bank of mist clings low to cement port holdings and the stalls of morning marketeers doing solemn business in the chill. A handful of modern schooners slip into and out of the harbor. They dwarf the hawkers and two figures, a tweedy HISTORIAN and his STUDENT, on the seawall looking out.

> **STUDENT**
> You're sure this is the place, Professor? It looks kind of …

> **HISTORIAN**
> Dismal? Dangerous? Legends come from places like this.

> **STUDENT**
> … dull.

> **HISTORIAN**
> … and they disappear here as well.

> **STUDENT**
> I think my contacts are frozen.

He withdraws deep into his jacket, blinks uncomfortably.

> **STUDENT (CONT'D)**
> Maybe he's not coming today?

> **HISTORIAN**
> He'll be here. This is his town.

> **STUDENT**
> You don't really believe ...?

> **HISTORIAN**
> You don't really believe.

The two of them look at each other and laugh, turning the icy air into mist.

> **STUDENT**
> Look –

> **HISTORIAN**
> No, look.

The historian points towards the head of the harbor. The mist pushes away, fading before an old sailed schooner and on its deck, the suntanned figure of THE LAST EXPLORER.

EXT. THE EXPLORER'S SHIP – KING'S LYNN – DAY

Swaggering the length of his ship, he laughs – a crackling sound that echoes profoundly.

> **THE EXPLORER**
> Floating above and not below, that's
> me! Another voyage, another return
> to my home away from home.
> King's Lynn, the lake on the sea!

He blows kisses to the HARBORMEN as his ship glides towards the narrow quay.

EXT. FREEZING QUAY – KING'S LYNN – DAY

The student rolls his eyes, but can't keep them away for long.

EXT. THE EXPLORER'S SHIP – KING'S LYNN – DAY

The Explorer bounds across the deck and picks up a glittering stone.

> **THE EXPLORER**
> I've been to the corner of the Earth
> and cut it like a diamond, to the
> oceanic ridge where the bones of
> the world lie exposed to the winds
> of time.

He tosses it carelessly over his shoulder, seizing instead: a whalebone.

> **THE EXPLORER (CONT'D)**
> I have wine made from the Rhine
> and the rind of Adam's apple.
> Treasures from around the world!
> Stories to tell of capture and escape,
> maps and charts to make your
> journeys safe!

EXT. FREEZING QUAY – KING'S LYNN – DAY

The Historian grins at the Student.

> **HISTORIAN**
> Well?

STUDENT
All I see is some old sailor who's
clearly been round the bend.

HISTORIAN
(his smile deepening)
He's been round many.

Harbormen tie up the Explorer's little ship. The Explorer climbs unsteadily up onto the pier before a small CROWD and wobbles on sea legs.

THE EXPLORER
The ship's in! The Ship's Inn! Take
me to the Ship's Inn! Now that I'm
on land I find I want to get wet!

INT. THE SHIP'S INN – KING'S LYNN – THAT NIGHT

Out of happy revelry and songs, like for a holiday, staggers The Explorer, drunk.

He collapses into an overstuffed chair by the lit fire, and gazes marvelously at the ongoing celebrations.

DRUNK SAILOR
Another story!

ANOTHER DRUNK SAILOR
Another beer! Cheers.

THE EXPLORER
No, no. Friends, no. I just want to
listen to the songs for a while, here
by myself. I haven't spoken to so
many fish for hours!

A few laughs give way to resumed music and the uneven lyrics of the Singing Postman's *You Can't Keep Livin' in the Past*. The singers form a wheel, spinning too quickly for the drunk Historian.

He stumbles out of it and plops into the chair next to the Explorer. The Historian frowns deeply.

> **THE EXPLORER (CONT'D)**
> Ha, ha! Don't worry.
> (hiccups)
> You'll get back in.

> **HISTORIAN**
> It's the wheel of time.

The Explorer pauses, frowns up at the celebrations.

> **THE EXPLORER**
> Is that what they call it these days?

> **HISTORIAN**
> Isn't it beautiful?

> **THE EXPLORER**
> Well, yes.

> **HISTORIAN**
> It's horrible.

The Historian sniffles drunkenly, a damp sound underneath the revelry.

> **THE EXPLORER**
> Hey – now! You're drunk.

> **HISTORIAN**
> Listen to me. Listen to me! I'm an

historian, a modern man. I have to go back in there. But you don't have to. Keep exploring the small, the hidden places. They think there's nothing else out there to discover, but you know better. Modern men like me can only see the mundane in you, but I know who you are! You're the last explorer!

The Explorer laughs uproariously.

THE EXPLORER
The last! You're drunk, my friend!

HISTORIAN
All the better.

THE EXPLORER
I'm not the last! There are thousands more like me. All it takes to be an explorer is an open mind.

HISTORIAN
All the others have vanished. They came from their ports of call; they sailed, they walked, they flew from all the secret places to the city, the Dean's lure dangled before them.

THE EXPLORER
The Dean? Who?

The two drunk SAILORS disembark from the circle and, laughing, pick up the Historian by the arms.

> **DRUNK SAILOR 1**
> Come on, fella!

> **DRUNK SAILOR 2**
> You're missing out on all the fun!

> **DRUNK SAILOR 1**
> Come have one on me!

> **THE EXPLORER**
> Wait! Who's the Dean? The Dean of what?

> **HISTORIAN**
> The Dean –

The sailors haul him out of the chair and towards the circle. The Historian cranes his head around and looks back at the Explorer, his face a picture of TERROR. The sailors laugh and laugh.

> **THE EXPLORER**
> At least tell me where they went!

He tries to get up, but the Historian's gone, vanished among the dancing and the songs.

EXT. FREEZING QUAY – KING'S LYNN – NIGHT

A quick BLACK FIGURE slips on the frozen pier then, more carefully, crawls into the Explorer's ship.

INT. THE EXPLORER'S SHIP – KING'S LYNN – NIGHT

The figure opens one of the many chests and trunks in the Explorer's hold. It is the student, a torch jammed into his mouth.

He examines the contents: a hollow stone egg – hatched, a faerie wand, an alchemist's beaker still filled with gold ... He stuffs each one into his backpack.

> **STUDENT**
> Fake. Fake. What rubbish. Maybe you can fool these backwards people and my backwards professor, but not me. I'll prove you for a fake. I'll prove you for a liar!

> **THE EXPLORER (O.S.)**
> I'll prove him wrong! Says I'm the last. I can't be the last, he'll see.

The student slips behind a totem pole just as the Explorer lights a lamp in the open doorway. He walks right past the student and the open chest. Luckily, he's concentrating too hard to notice.

> **THE EXPLORER (CONT'D)**
> I'll find them out there. On the waves. In the secret places modern men don't dare. An explorer exploring for explorers, there's a first. Not a last!

He grabs a push-pole from a stack of equipment then heads back on deck.

EXT. THE EXPLORER'S SHIP – KING'S LYNN – NIGHT

At the side of the boat, the Explorer unties the mooring, then pushes off with the pole.

Behind him, in the dim lantern light from the open door of the hold, the student leaps off the ship onto the pier.

As The Explorer pushes his sailing ship along, he turns to watch the lights of King's Lynn retreat down the river – the lanterns of the Inn, the docking lights, the signals on the tall cranes, the stars reflected in the water.

Among them all glitter two more pins of light. He doesn't notice them – but up close they are unmistakable. They're the contact lenses in the Student's EYES.

EXT. KING'S LYNN – DAY

Early morning over King's Lynn. Fog grows on the city like mold on bread. Shouts and conversation, cars in the street making rivers to the sea.

EXT. FREEZING QUAY – KING'S LYNN – NIGHT

The student struggles against a current of sailors and harbormen carrying tools and rope. He's clumsy under his bulging backpack, sometimes bumping into people as he squints up at each face he passes.

> **STUDENT**
> Professor? Have you seen my
> history professor? He went to the
> inn last night with …
> (doesn't know what to say)
> Excuse me. Have you seen …?

> **STUDENT (CONT'D)**
> He was wearing a kind of tweed
> coat, so tall, brown eyes …

One of the drunk sailors from last night frowns at him, shakes his head.

> **DRUNK SAILOR**
> Sorry. Haven't seen anyone like that.

The student stumbles out of the way. He blinks miserably, puts contact solution in his eyes from a bottle. It streams down his face. He brushes the drops away irritably.

STUDENT
The fool!

INT. THE SHIP'S INN – KING'S LYNN – DAY

The student wanders into the cozy room looking for his tutor. It's empty save for an ANCIENT MAN in tweeds in an overstuffed chair near the fire.

STUDENT
Excuse me, have you seen …

He stops, peers at the man, who looks back uncomprehendingly. Despite the wrinkled skin and the vacant expression, it's clearly the Historian. The student doesn't recognize him.

STUDENT (CONT'D)
Where did you get that jacket?

HISTORIAN
I don't remember. I used to be
quite good with history, you know.
Is it yours?

STUDENT
It belongs to my professor. He was
here last night. He must have left
it behind.

The student reaches out to take it from him, but the old man recoils.

HISTORIAN
It's cold!

STUDENT
Well ... if you find him, would you tell him that I've gone back to the University alone? And that I've got some stuff that proves he's been wasting his time with all this explorer nonsense. And ... oh, never mind!

HISTORIAN
Never mind! Wasting time!
He he he.

The student digs around in his pocket and produces some change. He puts it in front of the old man.

STUDENT
Here. Have a beer to warm yourself up if you like.

The student steps out into the cold while the old man, once the historian, now history itself, stares sadly at the coins on the table.

HISTORIAN
Just one more, maybe.

Drew Castalia is an American with a Canadian writing degree and ambitions in the UK. His scripts represent a fascination with distorted visions, dreams, subliminal memes, and fantasy. More than ever, these are the things that unite us.

Ben Craib

Lovestruck

EXT. STREET – DAY

A switched-off iPod in a hand.

A finger presses play. The screen illuminates.

The finger finds 'Cover Flow' and moves round the circle, clockwise and anti-clockwise, flicking through thousands of songs.

Back and forth, back and forth, what is it looking for?

The finger belongs to MAN (thirtysomething, scruffy, hungover) standing at a bus stop, fiddling with his iPod.

The bus stop is on an unglamorous London street. The weather is grim. There's litter and traffic.

Finally, the cursor settles on something. Man presses play.

Music – the soundtrack – begins: Jazz with syncopated rhythm – just drums and bass, funky, slow, building …

The title of the song on the iPod reads: LOVESTRUCK.

Man sticks out a hand. A bus pulls up.

INT. BUS – THE TOP DECK – DAY

Man walks up the stairs. Half way up he freezes. WOMAN (thirty-something, smoker, overly made-up) is sitting behind the staircase.

They hold each other's gaze for ten whole seconds. Neither of them betrays any feeling.

Woman looks away first. Man carries on up the stairs, and sits down in front of her, on the opposite aisle. He puts his head against the window and looks outside. Gritty London rolls by.

Slowly he turns his head and looks at Woman. Woman keeps cool and looks out of the window. Man scans the rest of the bus: A HOODY listens to music on his phone. A FAT BUSINESS MAN is reading a magazine. A YOUNG WOMAN looks out of the window, chewing gum. All are lost in their own little world.

He turns back to the front and Woman immediately stares at him. Fidgety, he turns again and instantly Woman looks back out the window. This time, Man lingers on Woman, but she keeps her gaze firmly fixed outside. Eventually Man turns back round, and quick as a flash Woman stares at him again. Now Man looks out of the window and it's Woman's turn to linger on him. Suddenly, Man turns quickly, and again, they hold each other's eyes, this time for barely a second before Man looks to the front, disturbed.

Outside, a traffic light turns red. The bus stops.

Man looks at the other passengers.

Young woman makes a gesture as if to say 'Go on!'

Business Man widens his eyes as if to say 'Come on!'

Hoody raises his hands as if to say 'What the f*** are you doing?!'

Decisively, Man gets up and walks down the aisle.

He dances for Woman! The music EXPLODES!

Woman smiles – AND DANCES FOR HIM!

THEY BOTH DANCE TOGETHER! ON THE SEATS! OFF THE SEATS! IN THE AISLE! THE OTHER PASSENGERS JOIN IN! THEY ALL FINISH IN ONE JOYOUS, SYNCHRONISED MOMENT OF RAPTURE!

The traffic light goes green.

END DREAM SEQUENCE.

INT. BUS – DAY

Music back to normal.

Man is looking out of the window, lost in his head. He notices something outside. He looks back at Woman. She's not looking at him.

Man presses the bell. He gets up and walks down the aisle. Slowly and reluctantly he descends the stairs.

EXT. BUS – DAY

Man gets off the bus.

He looks up at the window, longing.

Woman looks back at him.

She smiles. He smiles. The bus drives off.

THE END

Ben Craib is a twenty-seven-year-old scriptwriter currently studying on the Creative Writing MA at the University of East Anglia, where he is developing a full-length play. His previous play, *Teenage Love in Twisted Dreamland*, was a winner of Menagerie Theatre Company's SPARKS competition and received a reading at The Junction, Cambridge in January 2009.

Chris Duffill

Multiple
An extract from part one of a four-part television thriller

ACT ONE

INT. EXECUTIVE RESTROOM, SANDERSON OIL HQ – DAY

JANINE BAXTER (36) studies her reflection in a wall of mirror-glass. She's wearing a smart grey trouser-suit. She's pretty – but her expression is blank, her eyes void of emotion. The restroom is polished marble and glass, some cubicles, a short row of shiny white sinks. She straightens an ID badge on her jacket; it reads: 'Star Office Temps: SALLY DAVIS'. On automatic pilot, she applies her lipstick.

INT. EXECUTIVE FLOOR, SANDERSON OIL HEADQUARTERS – DAY

Baxter emerges from the restroom and sits behind a secretary's desk. The spacious office is plush and modern. A polished steel sign on a nearby wall reads: 'SANDERSON OIL (UK)'. A frosted glass door with the sign 'Gerald Sanderson, CEO' is behind her. A speakerphone beeps.

> SANDERSON (O.S.) *(via speakerphone)*
> Miss Davis, would you come
> in please.

INT. GERALD SANDERSON'S OFFICE – DAY

Traditional decor clashes with the modern building. GERALD SANDERSON (54) sits behind a large antique desk. Well-groomed in a dark blue suit, there's an air of arrogance about him. Baxter enters. Her expression is fixed.

      SANDERSON
    Miss Davis, did I not make myself
    clear? Coffee. Nine a.m. sharp.

Baxter nods blankly.

      SANDERSON (CONT'D)
    Well? Snap to it.

INT. OUTSIDE GERALD SANDERSON'S OFFICE – DAY

Pouring coffee, Baxter's hand shakes, she's sweating. She removes a fountain pen from her pocket and places it on a tray next to the coffee cup. A look of horror flashes over her face, then anger. The blank look returns.

INT. GERALD SANDERSON'S OFFICE – DAY

Baxter enters. Busy on paperwork, Sanderson doesn't look up.

      SANDERSON
    Just put it on the desk.

Baxter approaches Sanderson with the tray.

      BAXTER
    Overbearing bastard.

      SANDERSON
    What the devil –

> **BAXTER**
> (sweetly)
> Your nine a.m. coffee, Sir?

Baxter pours the coffee onto the desk. Before he can react, she drops the tray and lunges at Sanderson with the pen. He recoils, scrambles out of his chair.

> **SANDERSON**
> Christ!

Baxter grips the pen tightly. She stops moving. The cold sweat returned, she wrestles with her own mind.

> **BAXTER**
> (to herself)
> Please. Please don't.

> **SANDERSON**
> Don't what!?

> **BAXTER**
> Shut up!

She looks at Sanderson with tortured eyes.

> **BAXTER (CONT'D)**
> I'm sorry.

Sanderson runs for the door. She charges at him, holding the pen like a knife. He spins around, raises his arms to defend himself. She slams into him. The two fall backwards and Baxter loses her grip on the pen – it rolls underneath a filing cabinet. Sanderson kicks Baxter away – she slams into his desk and collapses. He scrambles to his feet and dives for his phone.

> **SANDERSON**
> (to phone)
> Security!

Baxter stands and grabs a new pen from the desk. Sanderson backs off. The hate on Baxter's face suddenly melts away. Confounded, Sanderson watches as she slumps into his chair. Her eyes stare blankly into space.

INT. MEGAN'S OFFICE, MI5 HEADQUARTERS – DAY

TITLES over. MEGAN ROBERTS (37) sits bolt upright in a comfy leather chair. She has short bobbed hair, minimal make-up. A smart black trouser-suit undercuts her femininity and accents her angular build. The light in the office is heavily subdued by drawn blinds, the decor is modern and minimalist – a simple desk and PC in front of a full bookcase. Other than certificates on the wall, there are no personal effects.

Sitting opposite her is ALAN WEST (39). West has an ex-paratrooper look – tough, intelligent. His shoulders are hunched, he's nervous. Between them, on a low coffee table, are a couple of cups and a running dictaphone.

> **MEGAN**
> It's OK. You're off assignment. What you're experiencing isn't unusual.

West tentatively smiles.

> **WEST**
> What is it they say? If you think you're being watched –

> **MEGAN**
> You're probably working for MI5.

West smiles, reaches for coffee. His hand shakes.

Multiple

WEST
Look. I'm fine. Can't you just prescribe something?

MEGAN
I see ... I'm here to help you work through your issues, Alan. Not bury them under a stack of pills.

WEST
This is counter-intelligence, Roberts, not bloody traffic duty! Just give me the pills – you lot drug people all the time.

MEGAN
To aid in the interrogation of suspects – yes. But you're not a suspect, are you West?

WEST
Out come the old psychological thumbscrews. What? Think you've spotted some tell-tale sign of subterfuge?

MEGAN
This isn't an interrogation. I'm here to help you.

WEST
So you say. But I know. All MI5 shrinks have a remit to spot double-agents. You're wasting your time with me.

> **MEGAN**
> Calm down. If I were conducting any kind of interrogation on you you'd know about it.

> **WEST**
> Would I? Would I really?

> **MEGAN**
> Yes. Yes you would.

INT. HOSPITAL, MENTAL HEALTH ASSESSMENT UNIT – DAY

A ward in an ageing NHS building. It's eerily quiet. A WARD SISTER (42) is at a reception desk, a security door opposite. A bell sounds. The Ward Sister sees two POLICE OFFICERS outside. She buzzes the security door open. The officers enter, accompanied by TWO PARAMEDICS. They wheel Baxter inside on a trolley – she's sedated.

> **WARD SISTER**
> Hello. Who have we got here?

> **POLICE OFFICER #1**
> Sally Davis. Some secretary. Flipped out, attacked her boss.

The buzzer sounds again. BARCLAY (40), an officious fresh-faced man in a suit, waits outside with TWO MEDICS. The Ward Sister lets them in. The two medics commandeer Baxter from the startled ambulance crew.

> **PARAMEDIC**
> What do you think you're doing?

Barclay approaches the desk. He presents an MI5 ID.

Multiple

> **BARCLAY**
> I am authorised under section four
> of the Official Secrets Act to take
> custody of this woman.

> **POLICE OFFICER #2**
> I'll have to call this in.

> **BARCLAY**
> Do so. You'll find Chief Inspector
> Stevens has been informed. You will
> not include this woman, or events
> connected to her, in your report.
> Any breach of these instructions will
> constitute a threat to national
> security, an offence punishable
> under law. Is that understood?

The paramedics nod. The police officers look put out.

> **POLICE OFFICER #2**
> All right. No need to go overboard.

> **BARCLAY**
> Thank you for your co-operation.

Barclay follows the medics as they leave with Baxter. The Ward Sister and Paramedics look on, stunned.

> **POLICE OFFICER #1**
> M-I-bloody-Five.

EXT. HOSPITAL – DAY

A man in council worker's clothes smokes a cigarette near the entrance. He's CYPHER (50) – balding, a face like a wall of stone with sharp eyes chiselled into it. He watches as Barclay and the medics load Baxter into a private ambulance and drive away. Displeased, Cypher leaves.

INT. MEGAN'S OFFICE, MI5 HEADQUARTERS – DAY – LATER

Megan opens the blinds, letting in the sunlight; her office is empty. There's a knock, KATE WHITE (29) pops her head around the door. She's smart casual, professional, bright.

> **KATE**
> Megan, it's twelve-thirty. Thought you should know.

Megan checks her watch – kicks herself, she's late.

> **MEGAN**
> Oh God. Thanks Kate.

> **KATE**
> Tough morning?

> **MEGAN**
> You could say that.

> **KATE**
> Hey, I wish I had the afternoon off. Least you could do is smile. Go on, do it for me.

Megan breaks into a smile. Kate grins and leaves. Megan tidies the paperwork on her desk and unearths a small framed photo of her husband and young son. It's fallen over. She stands it up, grabs her keys and leaves.

INT. MEGAN'S APARTMENT, SOUTH BANK, LONDON – DAY

The open-plan apartment overlooks the Thames. Small but expensive, it's overrun with family life – a child's paintings in an art corner, toys in the living area, a busy kitchen. Kids' party music plays. A dining table set with party plates and balloons.

Megan is mixing a cake, hands covered in flour, still wearing her trouser-suit. JACOB ROBERTS (9) watches Megan excitedly. THOMAS ROBERTS (40) wobbles on a chair as he pins up a 'HAPPY 10th BIRTHDAY!' banner. Despite his slight build, Thomas's casual clothes hide a middle-age spread.

Megan spoons the mix into a tin – it splatters on her jacket. Jacob laughs. Megan slumps. Thomas climbs down to help.

      THOMAS
    Hey Jakey, want to finish your
    picture before the party?

      JACOB
    Yeaah!

Jacob runs to an easel and starts painting. Thomas smiles at the mess on Megan's jacket.

      THOMAS
    Home from work five minutes and
    look at the state of you.

      MEGAN
    OK 'Mummy'. Anyway, isn't this
    supposed to be your job?

Thomas shoots her a playful 'don't push me' look. She capitulates, smiles. He admires the banner.

      THOMAS
    Ten. Whatever happened to one-to-
    nine? The old 'time flies' cliché I s'pose.

Chris Duffill

> **MEGAN**
> Careful, don't get me started.

> **THOMAS**
> Ah yes, the inner workings of the
> temporal lobe by Megan Roberts,
> super-shrink. Fascinating stuff.

Megan smiles. Her mobile rings. She freezes, looks at Thomas. Jacob stops painting.

> **THOMAS (CONT'D)**
> Don't.

Megan takes out her phone. She hesitates, looks at Jacob. He's holding a painting of 'Daddy, me and a birthday cake'. The phone is still ringing. Thomas catches Megan's eye, he knows what's coming. She takes a deep breath and answers the phone.

> **MEGAN**
> (to phone)
> Megan Roberts.

EXT. MI5 BUILDING, LONDON – DAY

The MI5 building is a towering wall of stone, broken only by rows of small windows. Megan's car, a grey Audi coupé, pulls up at a security gate. A SECURITY OFFICER waves her into a basement car park.

INT. OBSERVATION BOOTH, MI5 HEADQUARTERS, LONDON – DAY

> **KATE**
> Janine Baxter. Listed as active. Been
> with MI5 six years.

Baxter struggles against her restraints.

> BARCLAY
> According to her ID badge she's
> Sally Davis, an office temp. Lucky for
> us Sanderson's security people
> found her mobile and called the
> 'home' number – came straight
> through to us. Otherwise we'd have
> lost her to a state institution.

JOHN FORRESTER (54) enters – a wise, distinguished face; comfortable in a charcoal three-piece suit. There's something of the 'British Establishment' about him.

> MEGAN AND KATE
> Sir.

Forrester looks through the glass at Baxter.

> FORRESTER
> This can't get out. A rogue MI5
> agent attacking the head of a major
> oil company? We'd never hear the
> end of it. I want this dealt with.

Megan opens a file.

> MEGAN
> (whilst reading)
> Baxter's last occupational therapy
> session was one month ago. There
> are some issues, stress, the usual,
> but no signs of anything like this.

Megan leans closer to the glass, studying Baxter.

                    MEGAN (CONT'D)
I'm going inside.

INT. PADDED CELL, MI5 HEADQUARTERS – DAY

The lights are low. Megan approaches Baxter.

                    MEGAN
I'm Megan – a friend, Janine.

                    BAXTER
I'm Sally.

                    MEGAN
All right, Sally. I'm on your side.

                    BAXTER
(fearful, to herself)
You're not supposed to be here.
(instantly 'normal')
Don't look so worried, I'm right as rain.

                    MEGAN
Sally, is Janine with you? Can I speak with her? Please?

                    BAXTER
She's not talking. She failed.

                    MEGAN
I know Janine. I know she's sorry. She's sorry she failed. Sally, it's important you tell her what she's failed to do. Tell her.

>   **BAXTER**
> We didn't get Sanderson!
> (a pause, confused)
> Cypher?

>   **MEGAN**
> Cypher?

Baxter suddenly looks confused, frightened.

>   **MEGAN (CONT'D)**
> OK, get Sanderson. Then what?
> (Baxter hesitates)
> It's all right. Janine just needs
> reminding, Sally. Then what?

>   **BAXTER**
> Take control.

With sudden violence, Baxter thrashes against her restraints.

>   **BAXTER (CONT'D)**
> Take control!

INT. CORRIDOR, MI5 HEADQUARTERS – DAY

Megan and Kate leave the observation booth and walk.

>   **MEGAN**
> Extreme multiple personality
> disorder. It doesn't develop
> overnight like that. I want bloods –
> toxicology, everything.

>   **KATE**
> I'll see to it.

> **MEGAN**
> Why only 'attack' Sanderson? If she'd wanted to kill him she could, she has the skill.

> **KATE**
> Perhaps Sanderson was part of Baxter's current assignment?

> **MEGAN**
> Perhaps. I'd say we have a need to know, wouldn't you?

INT. FORRESTER'S OFFICE, MI5 HEADQUARTERS – DAY

Forrester sits behind a glass-topped desk in a large executive office. Career memorabilia decorate the walls. A small name-plate on the desk reads 'Director of Operations'. Sitting opposite him, a respectable distance away, is Megan.

Forrester slides a file across the table. Megan opens it. Inside there's a PHOTO of a tall man with piercing eyes.

> **FORRESTER**
> Anton Vasiliev. A Russian agent at the centre of a spy ring that Baxter was trying to infiltrate. Vasiliev is known to have recruited several British agents. I've had it checked and verified – none of this has anything to do with Sanderson.

> **MEGAN**
> Why would Baxter go to the trouble of infiltrating Sanderson Oil if there isn't a connection?

FORRESTER
You suspect some 'foreign' influence over her actions?

MEGAN
It's possible. We're testing her for psychoactive drugs.

Forrester folds his arms, concern spreading on his face.

MEGAN (CONT'D)
Sir, this is either a product of a genuine psychosis, or Baxter was brainwashed by an outside agency. I can find out, given time, but I need more information.

FORRESTER
I see. Well, for now I think you should focus on your patient's immediate psychological needs. Leave the external investigation to our field agents.

MEGAN
But I can't begin to separate fact from fantasy unless I –

FORRESTER
We need to maintain tight control over the external investigation. Keep it low key. What'll happen if I let you loose out there? An MI5 psychologist asking questions all over London – the press will be onto it like a pack of wolves. And if they

manage to link Baxter to the attack on Sanderson ... Well, we'd have another parliamentary enquiry on our hands. And nobody wants that, hmm?

END OF EXTRACT

Chris Duffill graduated from Manchester with a Television Production degree in the early 90s. He went on to write scripts for independent production companies, eventually becoming a Creative Director and running a successful internet design agency. Chris is currently developing scripts for a TV serial and a feature film.

Jake Marcet

Summer Break
A children's TV show
Extract from 'June of the Penguins'

EXT. BERT ANDERNIE MIDDLE SCHOOL – DAY

A red-bricked middle school on a perfect, sunny day. An American flag flutters in the breeze.

>CHUCK (V.O.)
>The last day of school. You'd think
>that everyone would be happy with
>summer so close and school soon to
>be a distant memory.

INT. BERT ANDERNIE MIDDLE SCHOOL – DAY

The hallways are empty except for the sounds of the lectures from inside the classrooms. Peeking inside the doors one sees the completely oblivious faces of the students as the teachers drag on.

>CHUCK (V.O.)
>Scientists in Russia recently
>determined that students stand a
>78% greater chance of going insane
>on the last day of school as opposed
>to any other time in the year.

A GINGER BOY (11) leaps up from his seat. The OTHER STUDENTS, including a boy we will find out is ERIK PETERS (12), glance at him but keep their heads resting on their palms.

              GINGER BOY
        I can't take it! The clock! It! Hasn't!
        Moved! Time has stopped! We're
        trapped! Don't you see?! Trapped!

The teacher that we will later learn is MR POWERS (late 20s) doesn't even notice the distraction and keeps on teaching.

            GINGER BOY (O.S.)
        Escape with me!

              CHUCK (V.O.)
        Rumor has it that a classroom in
        Kenosha last year vanished. They
        just ... disappeared from time; stuck
        on the last day of school forever.

In another classroom, a student that we will find out is CHUCK PETERS (16) is staring intently at a clock. Its hands move slowly.

              CHUCK (V.O.)
        Every single student in this school
        right now is counting down the
        minutes, the seconds, the
        milliseconds, even the nano seconds
        until they can leave for the summer.
        Everyone, that is, but me.

A NERD (16) has an abacus on his desk and is moving beads, lost in his calculations. A BOY (16) is clutching at his desk, his legs, torso, and most of his upper body already out of the chair and on the way out the door.

> **CHUCK (V.O.)**
> Because this summer I wasn't just getting away from school, I was getting a job.

INT. PETERS HOUSE – KITCHEN – DAY

Chuck – gangly and awkward-looking – sits head-down at the kitchen table. Sitting at the table with him is his brother Erik. Erik is a rosy-cheeked youth. His hair immaculately parted. He looks like a businessman in training.

Erik is digging through his backpack and pulling out book after book, paper after paper and throwing them all into the trash. MOM (mid-40s) – a Martha Stewart-ish type – is in an apron and doing mom-sorts of things.

> **CHUCK**
> I just really don't see why I need a job now.

> **MOM**
> You're old enough, it's a sign of responsibility.

> **ERIK**
> (pulling textbooks from his bag; throwing them away)
> Boy am I glad I don't have any responsibilities.

Mom pats Erik on the head and gets back to doing her mom stuff.

> **CHUCK**
> I'm responsible, I can do things.
> I just really don't want to do this.

Jake Marcet

> **MOM**
> Well then I guess you really don't want to drive since you won't have any money for gas. Money doesn't grow on trees you know; your father and I think it's time that we stopped paying for you.

> **DAD (O.S.)**
> When I was your age I took every job I could find! I mowed lawns, I walked dogs –

> **CHUCK**
> But ... but ... I'm your baby!

Erik snickers and starts pulling out desk accessories: paper organizers, globes, a desk calendar.

> **DAD (O.S.)**
> – a lumberjack, an Associate Justice of the Supreme Court –

> **MOM**
> You are my baby. You're just my baby who needs a job. You really should be thankful that Mr Burton is letting you do this. Now, you're going to be late; run off and get changed.

Chuck heaves a sigh and exits.

> **DAD (O.S.)**
> – and a sherpa!

Mom finishes her work and sits down next to Erik. Erik has just pulled a projector and screen from his bag and thrown it away.

> **MOM**
> What about you, Erik? What are your plans for the summer?

> **ERIK**
> Oh, you know, the usual. Baseball games, the park, maybe go gigging for frogs –

> **MOM**
> Gigging for frogs?

> **ERIK**
> Yeah, all the kids do it now.

Erik pulls a circa-1980s computer from his bag and throws it away.

> **MOM**
> Was that a computer?

> **ERIK**
> Sure was, Mom.

> **MOM**
> (motions towards the can)
> Why'd you …?

> **ERIK**
> It had school cooties.

> **MOM**
> Right.

Chuck re-enters wearing a penguin costume. He looks like a college mascot if the college happened to be the Giant Sad Penguins. He looks pathetic.

Jake Marcet

> **CHUCK**
> (his voice muffled while in the costume)
> I hate my life.

> **MOM**
> Aw, you look adorable.

> **ERIK**
> I changed my mind Mom, I am going to spend all summer making fun of Chuck.

> **MOM**
> Hey now. Chuck is out earning money. You could learn something from him.

Chuck slumps his shoulders and, if possible, looks even more pathetic.

> **MOM**
> Come on, I'll give you a ride to work.

Mom leaves the house with Chuck walking slowly behind.

> **ERIK**
> (calling after him)
> I'm totally coming to visit you later!

EXT. CAR – DAY

Chuck is standing next to the door of the pickup truck. He can't open it. Mom comes around to open the door for him and goes back to the driver's side.

Chuck cannot fit in the door.

>   **MOM**
>   Well, this is a problem.

Chuck slumps even more.

EXT. ON THE ROAD – DAY – MOMENTS LATER

The pickup drives off with Chuck sitting sadly in the back.

INT. BURTON'S CINEMA – DAY

Burton's Cinema is a classic-looking movie house. Posters for classic movies, workers in ridiculous looking outfits, all the glamour and glitz of a retro movie theatre.

It is also empty of patrons.

Chuck walks up to the one man he can find. It is LEVAR BURTON (early 50s) – the actor who played Geordi from *Star Trek: The Next Generation*.

>   **CHUCK**
>   (voice still muffled by the suit)
>   Mr Burton?

LeVar Burton turns around and is not at all surprised to see a giant, sad penguin behind him.

>   **LEVAR BURTON**
>   Ah! Chuck! You're here!

>   **CHUCK**
>   Yes, sir.

Chuck starts to take the head off of the costume.

Jake Marcet

> **LEVAR BURTON**
> Whoa. Keep that on there, Chuck. Can't let the little kids see you outside of your character. It'd ruin the experience, you know?

Chuck looks around. The theatre is still empty.

> **LEVAR BURTON**
> Chuck, I'm not gonna lie to you: business has been pretty slow around here lately.

Chuck again looks around. The theatre is still empty, save for a tumbleweed that rolls on by.

> **LEVAR BURTON**
> So here's what I thought: what is it about a movie theatre that people love?

> **CHUCK**
> Um, the movies?

> **LEVAR BURTON**
> No! The air conditioning! It's hot outside, it's cold in here. It's sheer elegance in its simplicity, Chuck.

> **CHUCK**
> Is that why I'm a penguin?

> **LEVAR BURTON**
> (pats Chuck on the head)
> You're catching on, big guy. Now here, take this sign, and get to work.

LeVar Burton hands Chuck a sign that reads 'Cool Off at the Hottest Spot in Town!'.

EXT. PARKING LOT – DAY – MOMENTS LATER

Chuck is walking, head down through an empty parking lot, dragging his sign behind him.

> CHUCK (V.O.)
> Well, there it was. My summer vacation – my dignity – ruined because the blind guy from *Star Trek* had a new idea for a marketing strategy.

Chuck stops and looks at the sign he's carrying.

> CHUCK (V.O.)
> This isn't even funny. Who's going to listen to this? You know, I wanted to be an astronaut one day. No one ever made Neil Armstrong carry a sign like this. Gah. My life can't get any worse than it is right now.

> ERIK (O.S.)
> Step right up, ladies and gentlemen! See the world's saddest penguin!

> CHUCK (V.O.)
> Clearly, I was wrong.

EXT. STREET CORNER – DAY – CONTINUOUS

Standing on the street corner with a bullhorn is Erik. He's standing underneath a lemonade stand-looking booth that says 'See the boy with the life worse than yours!'

Jake Marcet

> **ERIK**
> Come one, come all! Taunt the penguin! Take pictures with him! Heck, you can even throw water balloons at him!

A CROWD materializes out of nowhere and starts to murmur.

> **CHUCK**
> Erik, what are you doing?

> **ERIK**
> Quiet, we can't let the marks know we know each other.

> **CHUCK**
> Marks ... I ... what is going on?

> **ERIK**
> Mom told me I should get a job, so I thought, what can a young entrepreneur like me do to make money?

> **CHUCK**
> So you're making fun of me?

> **ERIK**
> Not me, Chuck. To tell you the truth, I respect you for putting on the suit. No, what I'm doing is giving people an outlet for their own self-esteem problems. People will pay big money to realize that their life is better than someone else's.

          CHUCK
(sighs)
But who am I going to pay?

          ERIK
Huh?
(shushes Chuck)
Quiet. Customer.

A MAN (50s) comes up and starts talking to Erik. Chuck just holds up his banner for the movie theatre. His costume has never looked more pathetic than it does now.

          MAN
So, I can just, like, insult him?

          ERIK
For a price you can.

          MAN
How much to tell him he's ugly?

          ERIK
A popular choice indeed. Five dollars.

The man hems and haws and finally pulls his wallet from his pocket.

          CHUCK
I can't believe you're doing this to me.

          ERIK
Quiet! The customers are always right.

Jake Marcet

The man hands the five dollars over to Erik who makes a big show of counting it. Satisfied, he nods to the man.

The man steps up in front of Chuck, centers himself, takes a deep breath.

      MAN
   You are ugly.

Chuck just hangs his head.

The man smiles wide, and then walks away.

EXT. PARKING LOT – NIGHT

A LOVABLE GRANNY (80s) has just handed Erik a 10 dollar bill.

      GRANNY
   You will never amount to anything!

She grabs her walker and happily walks off. The lines are gone. It's just Chuck and Erik.

      ERIK
   We did it, brother! We raked in the
   money tonight!

      CHUCK
   You raked in the money tonight. I
   had Father O'Callahan tell me that
   there is no room in heaven for me.

      ERIK
   Ah, don't take it personally, the
   archbishop said you were only going
   to rot in purgatory for 10,000 years.
   There's hope.

> **CHUCK**
> Erik, I can't —

> **LEVAR BURTON (O.S.)**
> Hey!

Chuck and Erik turn around as LeVar Burton comes running over from the theatre.

> **CHUCK**
> It's 10pm Mr Burton, I'm heading home.

> **LEVAR BURTON**
> It's not you I want to talk to.

Erik makes a 'Who? Me?' face.

> **LEVAR BURTON**
> I saw what you were doing.

> **CHUCK**
> He's my brother ... can you just —

> **ERIK**
> (feigning tears)
> I'm so sorry! My mom told me to go and help out Chuck! I didn't know what I was doing! Please, don't —

> **LEVAR BURTON**
> I want a cut.

> **ERIK**
> (tears stop)
> What?

CHUCK
What?

LEVAR BURTON
You heard me. Chuck's my penguin. Theatre stayed pretty empty today. If you could funnel your penguin people into my theatre, I'll make it worth your while.

ERIK
Seems to me, it's worth my while already.

LEVAR BURTON
Let me put it this way, if you can't get the people in my theatre, I pull the penguin.

CHUCK
O thank you, Lord.

ERIK
Whoa, whoa, whoa. Let's not be hasty here.

CHUCK
Please, let's be hasty.

LEVAR BURTON
If you find a way to start getting the people out here into the movie theatre, I'll split the money you make 70/30.

ERIK
What! That's not fair at all! I had a good deal going here!

> **LEVAR BURTON**
> He's my penguin. Don't forget that.

> **CHUCK**
> (trying to butt in)
> Um, excuse me?

> **ERIK**
> 60/40.

> **LEVAR BURTON**
> 65/35.

> **CHUCK**
> Hello? Anyone?

> **ERIK**
> Deal.

LeVar Burton and Erik shake hands and walk away from each other. LeVar back towards the theatre and Erik off for home.

Chuck is left all alone standing on the sidewalk. A streetlight shines down on him. He slumps his shoulders.

> **CHUCK**
> I quit.

END OF EXTRACT

Jake Marcet studied poetry in the cornfields at Knox College, wrote sketch comedy with some very funny people at the iO Theatre, and came to England to learn he just wants to write TV. He hails from Chicago, Illinois.

UEA Creative Writing Anthology 2009

Ruth Selwyn-Crome

Bonfire Night

EXT. BELFAST – OPEN FIELDS BY A BUSY ROAD – 11PM – NOVEMBER 5TH 2008

A match is lit. A hand moves down to light a piece of faded brown floral 30s material, which flares up immediately.

A large old-fashioned armchair burns fierce and bright in the darkness.

INT. FRANK'S BEDROOM – 6AM – SAME DAY

A faint sound of an Underworld track pulses out. A bedside alarm beeps over the other sounds. It's pitch black apart from an alarm flashing beside FRANK (50), asleep.

Frank's eyes open and he reaches over to switch on a sidelight and switch off the alarm. He has greying black hair which is sticking up in clumps around headphones in his ears. He is wiry and pale. He looks very tired.

Frank pulls out the headphones. Slightly louder Underworld thumps out from them.

The room is cramped and badly decorated; dominated by a wall of modern stereo equipment.

INT. BATHROOM – CONTINUOUS

Frank, in long johns, stands in front of a tatty mirror and a square, 30s sink, above which is a shelf full of medicine bottles, white boxes of prescription pills and a tube of dentures fixative.

Frank picks out a tube of 'ROCKHARD' Hair Gel from behind the medicines, squirts a large dollop onto his hand, then smoothes it through his hair into a slicked-back style. Frank holds first one nostril then the other as he clears his sinuses with a loud prolonged sniff.

INT. LANDING – CONTINUOUS

Frank stands in an 80s grey suit outside a shut bedroom door on the dingy landing. He opens the door and stares at an enormous wooden wardrobe packed to the brim with dark, 30s men's suits, one of which is pressed and hung on the inside of the door.

INT. HALLWAY – CONTINUOUS

Frank glances at the 30s-style sitting room through a doorway as he leaves carrying a briefcase.

The floral armchair from earlier sits in the window bay.

Frank checks his watch and his tie and sees the chair reflected in the large hallway mirror on the wall.

A large, brown, mantle clock gives out eight chimes.

EXT. FRANK'S CAR – CONTINUOUS

Frank drives past open fields in a brand new Golf. The fields are empty apart from a large sign advertising a forthcoming housing development. Graffiti on it says: REAL IRA.

INT. FRANK'S CAR – CONTINUOUS

Extremely loud electronic music thumps from the car stereo to which Frank doesn't show any reaction.

EXT. HIGH STREET – CONTINUOUS

Frank sits in his car in a traffic jam in a crowded suburban high street. Beside him is a large shop window where a bright lime green retro 60s chair sits, spotlit and alone apart from a backdrop of semi-transparent orange circular discs suspended from chains.

Two bored SCHOOLBOYS (13) sit with a badly assembled 'Guy' and a sign which reads:

INSERT

Bonfire party at St Collam's Tonight. 8pm. All proceeds to Church roof. Entry £5

BACK TO SCENE

A young, female SHOPPER passes by, glancing down at the guy.

SHOPPER
Sure enough, that's a sin.

SCHOOLBOY 1
No it's not, it's a sign!

Frank looks at the boys from inside his car.

SCHOOLBOY 2
Hey mister! Penny for the guy!

Frank smiles and drives on.

INT. FRANK'S OFFICE – 5PM

Frank stands behind a bland grey desk in a room with glass panels on two sides.

Through the glass office workers pack up for the day in a much larger, open plan office.

COLEEN (38) plump, stands opposite Frank.

> **COLEEN**
> So what do you think?

> **FRANK**
> It's SMT tomorrow. We need to get those spreadsheets ready.

> **COLEEN**
> I mean he's pretty much told me we're over.

Coleen starts to cry.

> **COLEEN**
> It wasn't my fault! I just did it for a laugh, you know?

Frank hands over a box of tissues. Coleen grabs one.

> **COLEEN**
> I don't suppose you're on Facebook. It's only a word isn't it? 'Single'. I knew it was a mistake. Never let your family and definitely not your husband onto your profile. They can spy on you then. It's, 'Who's Gavin

then?' and I'm like, 'I don't know! He's a new friend!', you know? He's just taken it the wrong way.

> **FRANK**
> Can't you delete it or something?

Coleen looks at Frank aghast.

> **COLEEN**
> My whole profile? All my friends? You got any idea how many people I'm friends with? Anyway, my friend Caz and me, we pretended to be this woman wanting to have no strings sex. Sent him a message this morning. I'll see if he bites then I've got him.

Frank puts on his jacket.

> **COLEEN**
> You visiting your mum tonight then?

Frank looks at his watch.

> **FRANK**
> Yes.

> **COLEEN**
> She. Well, is she going to come home do you think?

Coleen's mobile goes off.

Frank points at his watch and deftly leaves.

> **COLEEN**
> (into phone)
> Oh. He said yes did he? No. I'm not
> going to the bonfire party. It's OK
> Caz. I'm fine. Bye.

Coleen is devastated.

EXT. CAR PARK – 5.30PM – MOMENTS LATER

Frank marches towards the car. His mobile goes off and he answers, still walking.

> **FRANK**
> (into phone)
> Frank Carthy.

Solemn quiet talking comes from Frank's phone.

Frank stops walking.

> **FRANK**
> Where is she now?

The talking from the phone continues.

> **FRANK**
> She wanted O'Neill's. Stewartstown.
> Do I need to ring them or ... ?
> Thank you. Thank you for
> everything you've done for her.

Frank carefully opens and sits in his car. Very still.

INT. FRANK'S CAR – CONTINUOUS

Coleen taps loudly on the window.

> **COLEEN**
> Are you going through town?

Frank nods.

> **COLEEN**
> You're not going to visit your mum?

Frank looks up and winds the window down.

> **FRANK**
> No.

Frank opens the passenger door. Coleen gets in and sobs suddenly.

Frank starts the car and Underworld blares out. Frank quickly turns the stereo off.

> **FRANK**
> Is it late night closing tonight?

EXT. FRANK'S HOUSE – 9PM

Frank and Coleen pull up outside a terraced Victorian house in his car. The bright green chair from Habitat sits on top, precariously fixed with rope.

Frank and Coleen fall out of the car. Clearly, they've been drinking.

Frank undoes one of the ropes and the chair nearly falls off at once.

> **COLEEN**
> How're we gonna get it in?

INT. HALLWAY – MOMENTS LATER

Frank and Coleen force the green chair into the sitting room. It's obviously heavy.

> **COLEEN**
> You know how to show a girl a good time!

INT. FRANK'S SITTING ROOM – MOMENTS LATER

Frank switches on the light.

The green chair sits in the middle of the room.

> **COLEEN**
> (giggling)
> It looks fantastic.

Frank looks up at the mantelpiece. The mantel clock ticks loudly. A large pewter urn sits beside a picture of a MAN (40) dressed in one of the suits from the wardrobe, grinning with slicked back hair.

> **FRANK**
> I'll get the kettle on.

Coleen looks disparagingly at the large floral chair. Coleen's mobile goes off. She plonks down into the green chair.

> **COLEEN**
> (into phone)
> O my god Caz. You'll never believe where I am. Frank Carthy's. In his house. It's like the Rue Morgue. We just had a few drinks and one thing led to another and we ended up in Habitat.

Frank arrives behind her with two cups and saucers.

> **COLEEN**
> He's there is he? Yeah. Well, good luck to him.
> (pause)
> No, honestly I'm going to be all right.
> (sotto voce)
> I think he's gay actually.

Frank looks at the floral chair.

> **FRANK**
> I need your help.

INT. FRANK'S SITTING ROOM – MOMENTS LATER

The floral chair moves up and down.

Frank cries out.

Coleen and Frank emerge from behind the chair, dishevelled and sweaty. The chair is wedged diagonally between the bay and the new green chair.

> **COLEEN**
> We'll never get it out this way.

> **FRANK**
> Stay there and push from behind.

The mantel clock ticks loudly.

> **FRANK**
> One more push.

Coleen pushes the floral chair and Frank pushes the green chair until both chairs face each other – side by side.

The mantel clock gives out 10 chimes. It's 10pm.

The hallway is dark.

          COLEEN
    Frank. I've got to get going.

A thump comes from upstairs. Frank looks up anxiously.

          COLEEN
    Really Frank. I have to get back now.
    It's been ... fun. We'll have to do it
    again.

Frank grabs her hand.

          FRANK
    Just one more thing, Coleen.

Coleen smooths down her hair and pulls her stomach in.

          COLEEN
    Frank.

EXT. FRANK'S HOUSE – MOMENTS LATER

Frank and Coleen pull the floral chair out of the house.

A car skids to a halt beside the house and TOM (37) jumps out.

          TOM
    So this is why you changed it!

> **COLEEN**
> Tom! What're you talking about? O for God's sake. Will you listen to him!

Tom marches up to Frank. He tries to grab at him but the chair is between them on the path.

> **TOM**
> Been seeing my missus on the side have you? Nice, cosy little lunchtimes I suppose is it?

Coleen runs up to them.

> **COLEEN**
> You replied.

> **TOM**
> What? What you talking about?

> **COLEEN**
> 'No Strings Sex'. Ring any bells?

> **TOM**
> I'm always getting invites. I just press yes to get rid of them.

> **COLEEN**
> Well you said yes to me. But it wasn't me was it?

> **TOM**
> I wasn't thinking straight. You set your profile status to single so ...

Frank leans on the floral chair under a streetlamp.

> **FRANK**
> I don't give a flying fuck whatever the fucking status anybody is.

Tom and Coleen look surprised.

> **FRANK**
> My mother died this afternoon.

Tom and Coleen look contrite and awkward.

Frank looks at the house. The silhouette of the green chair sits in the bay. Fireworks are being set off somewhere nearby.

> **FRANK**
> I'm going to have a bonfire.

> **TOM**
> You need a hand there, then?

All four lift the chair reverentially onto the car.

EXT. BELFAST – OPEN FIELDS BY A BUSY ROAD – 6PM – NOVEMBER 5TH 2008

Tom, Coleen and Frank carry the floral chair through the darkness.

The schoolboys from earlier poke a dying fire nearby.

> **SCHOOLBOY 1**
> Hey mister! You're not allowed any dumping!

> **TOM**
> You show a bit of respect! His mother's dead.

The schoolboys follow the parade.

The chair is put down.

Frank pours petrol onto the chair and stands back.

Frank hesitates then lights a match.

Tom genuflects, followed by the schoolboys.

The floral chair burns as Coleen, Frank and Tom stand round solemnly.

Frank looks up at the sky. Fireworks are being let off all around.

FADE OUT

Ruth Selwyn-Crome was brought up in Lowestoft. She briefly trained at Camberwell Art School before moving back to Suffolk with her young son. She has had two stage plays produced (Eastbound 2002 and Pulse Festival 2003). She writes and performs poetry and has been published by Black Shed Press in New Zealand. Currently Ruth is interested in writing for TV.

William Simpson

Did the Eggs Break?

INT. BATHROOM, FARMHOUSE – MORNING, SUMMER 1947

A boy's hand turns a tap. It spits out rust-coloured water. As the flow steadies, the redness fades.

A cup on the basin holds three toothbrushes. The boy takes one, rinses it and applies toothpaste.

IN THE MIRROR

LEIGH (10) stares at himself. His hair is a thatch of brown. He wears a short-sleeved shirt, dull coloured, a tank top over it.

His eyes stray to a shelf by the mirror where a man's shaving kit gathers dust.

Leigh finishes brushing his teeth.

INT. KITCHEN – MORNING

Leigh's brother MICHAEL (5) kneels on a chair at the table drawing with crayons.

Leigh pours a glass of water from a jug on the counter. He looks out of the WINDOW:

Across the lawn, in the yard, a tractor idles, and Leigh can see his mother, EVE (early 30s), speaking with a LABOURER.

Leigh takes his drink to the table where he looks at Michael's drawing.

> **LEIGH**
> A pig's only got four legs, Michael. See? You've drawn one, two, three, four, five, six legs.

> **MICHAEL**
> It's a special pig.

Leigh walks towards the door.

> **MICHAEL**
> Where you going? Leigh?

EXT. YARD – CONTINUOUS

Leigh closes the back door. By the red-brick sheds, his mother gives instructions to the labourer.

> **LEIGH**
> Mother?

She waves at him: 'go away.'

He turns to a side-gate and heads through it.

EXT. LANE – LATER

Leigh wanders along, swiping with a stick at the grass growing beside the road.

A familiar chug-chug-chug. Leigh looks back as a tractor passes him.

                    LEIGH
          Morning!

THE LABOURER behind the wheel nods. Leigh watches the tractor trundle on then throws his stick. It falls well short.

EXT. FIELD – MORNING

Leigh scales a gate and lands with a squelch in the mud on the other side. He looks up at the field, tall with barley, and beyond it, a dark wood.

EXT. WOOD – LATER THAT MORNING

Leigh climbs a tree. As he reaches for another branch, through the leaves he sees, not far away, TWO MEN:

One is tall: ROBERT (mid-30s). His face is gaunt and covered in patches of stubble. The other man TOM (late 20s) is stocky and dark haired, with a broad, pock-marked face. The pair are dressed in clothes that do not fit.

Robert rants at the other man, jabbing his finger before stalking away through the trees. Tom stands a moment, before erupting in anger. He grabs a branch from the ground and hurls it against a tree.

Leigh leans forward.

It is at this moment that he loses his footing and plunges through the leaves to the ground below.

EXT. WOOD – CONTINUOUS

On the ground. A man's bare feet stand close by. Leigh looks up at Tom.

Tom grunts. Whether it is a grunt of amusement or anger is less clear.

William Simpson

                    TOM
            You got a nest up there?

Leigh shakes his head. Tom offers a hand and hauls Leigh up.

                    TOM
            You're all right. What's your name?

                    LEIGH
            Leigh.

                    TOM
            Want to help gather some wood?

EXT. CAMP, WOOD – DAY

Leigh gathers wood. Nearby, Tom tends to a small fire.

                    LEIGH
            What were you arguing about? You
            and the other man.

                    TOM
            Chickens.

                    LEIGH
            We don't have chickens. Just crops.

                    TOM
            Some people round here keep
            chickens.

Leigh approaches and drops his pile of wood on the ground. He sits beside Tom, who pokes at the fire.

Did the Eggs Break?

Leigh cannot help noticing the scars on Tom's arms. Tom cannot help noticing Leigh's gaze.

>   **TOM**
> Germans.

>   **LEIGH**
> You were a soldier?

Tom nods.

>   **LEIGH (CONT'D)**
> What's it like? Is it like the pictures?

>   **TOM**
> Yeah. Just like.

>   **LEIGH**
> My father died. He wasn't a soldier,
> he just died. No one talks about it.

They concentrate on the fire in silence a moment.

>   **LEIGH**
> I'm not sure I want to be a soldier.

Tom smiles.

>   **TOM**
> Me neither. What was your father
> like?

William Simpson

> **LEIGH**
> Sometimes I think I might forget. He let me drive the tractor. I steered and he did the pedals. We crashed once, but he said it was just him and Mother shouted at him. Mother doesn't let me drive.

> **TOM**
> Sounds like a good man.

Leigh smiles.

> **ROBERT (O.S.)**
> (singing)
> ... and he didn't mind the quack quack and the legs all dangling down-o, down-o, down-o, he didn't mind the quack quack and the legs all dangling down-o ...

Leigh and Tom turn to see Robert with a dead chicken in each hand.

> **ROBERT**
> I see we both brought friends! Ha! I'm Robert.

> **LEIGH**
> Leigh.

> **ROBERT**
> What was that, lad? You'll have to speak up.

> **TOM**
> His name's Leigh.

ROBERT
Old friends are you? Tom told you a lot about us, I suppose.

An exchange of looks between Robert and Tom. Satisfied, Robert sits beside Leigh and begins to pluck one of the chickens.

TOM
No problems?

ROBERT
No, no, I told you. People round here are very accommodating. You live nearby, Leigh?

LEIGH
Yes. My mother's farm.

ROBERT
I wish I'd grown up on a farm. I grew up in a city. You ever been to a city, Leigh? You ever been to London?

LEIGH
(shakes head)
I'd like to see it.

ROBERT
Lots of opportunities there for a young man, provided he's enterprising of course. Are you enterprising?

Leigh nods.

> ROBERT (CONT'D)
> A grown-up lad, I'd say. One who can be trusted. Am I right? Course I'm right.

> TOM
> Rob, don't –

> ROBERT
> What? Stop mumbling. I'm half deaf, you see, Leigh, it's a terrible affliction, a mighty burden.
> (to TOM)
> Now what was that, mate?

He grips the chicken. Tom says nothing.

> ROBERT (CONT'D)
> You see these clothes we bought? They don't fit us so well. And we're half starved. Tom gets ever so hungry, don't you, Tom? So if you can see your way to helping us on those counts ... You can do that for us, can't you? We're mates, aren't we?

Leigh looks at Tom, then nods.

INT. PARENTS' BEDROOM – LATER

Leigh opens a drawer. A man's clothes lie folded inside. He hesitates. On top of the chest of drawers is a photograph of his mother and father on their wedding day.

He looks at the photo. He changes his mind. Leigh closes the drawer.

Did the Eggs Break?

INT. KITCHEN – LUNCHTIME

Leigh and Michael eat sandwiches, while their mother puts various cakes and meals into a basket. Michael bangs his hands on the table.

> EVE
> Stop that.
> (to LEIGH)
> You look after your brother?

Leigh nods. Eve kisses her two sons on the forehead.

> MICHAEL
> I don't want you to go.

> EVE
> Sweetie, I have to go over to Mrs Kendrick, you know Mrs Kendrick? She's had a fall getting the eggs in from the hens. When somebody's hurt and they need us, don't you think we should help? We should, shouldn't we?

Michael is silent.

> EVE
> Good boy.

She goes. A moment later the back door slams.

> MICHAEL
> Did the eggs break?

Leigh considers his mother's words a moment before pushing his chair from the table.

INT. BACK HALL – LATER

Leigh ties up some of his father's clothes in paper with string. He adds a loaf of bread to the package.

He is watched by Michael.

                LEIGH
        You stay here.

                MICHAEL
        Mummy said –

                LEIGH
        Just stay here.

He goes out the door.

EXT. THE DEN – AFTERNOON

Tom and Robert put on their new clothes. Leigh waits, poking at the fire with a stick.

                ROBERT
        What about the food, you bring
        that?

                TOM
        It's here.

Robert snatches the loaf from Tom and, ripping off a chunk, devours it.

                TOM
        You get in any trouble?

> LEIGH
> No.

> ROBERT
> And you didn't tell no one? Good lad. Nice shirt this.

> TOM
> It was his father's.

> ROBERT
> (to LEIGH)
> Dead is he?

Leigh nods.

> ROBERT (CONT'D)
> And no step-daddy?

> LEIGH
> She wouldn't do that.

> ROBERT
> Course not, course not.

Robert looks up suddenly.

> ROBERT (CONT'D)
> Brought a mate, have you?

Leigh turns. Standing nearby is his confused brother.

> LEIGH
> Michael!

          MICHAEL
Who are they?

          LEIGH
They're ... friends. I told you to stay at home.

          ROBERT
Oh yeah, we're all mates here. Quite the picture of domesticity. Come on, little fellow, sit down with us.
(to LEIGH)
Your brother, is it? He looks like you.

          MICHAEL
No, I don't!

          ROBERT
No, you're much better looking aren't you?

Robert winks at Leigh.

          MICHAEL
Are you elves? Elves live in the wood.

          ROBERT
Are we elves? Are we, Tom? Ha.
(to LEIGH)
Here, Leigh, our fire's getting low. My feet are awful sore, you mind going for some wood?

Leigh hesitates.

> ROBERT
> Doesn't your mother tell you to do
> what grown-ups ask? Good lad,
> good lad.

Leigh stands.

EXT. WOODS, SHORT DISTANCE FROM THE CAMP – MINUTES LATER

Leigh gathers wood. He glances back to where Robert can be seen talking with Michael. Michael is playing with a twig. Tom tends to the fire, eyes down.

EXT. CAMP, WOOD – DAY

Leigh approaches the camp from behind. Robert has his back to him, but Leigh can hear the conversation. He kneels in the undergrowth and listens.

> ROBERT
> Good mates with His Majesty, we
> are, ha, if not each other. We've
> been his guests, in a manner of
> speaking.

> MICHAEL
> Can I be a guest of His Majesty?

> ROBERT
> One day, my boy, maybe. If you
> promise to help me. Your house a
> big house, is it, Michael, with lots of
> lovely things in it?

> MICHAEL
> Yes.

William Simpson

Tom glances up from the fire. He cannot help seeing Leigh, who looks back with alarm.

>   **ROBERT**
> Big windows, big door. Big lock?

Leigh stares at Tom. He must have seen him ...

>   **MICHAEL**
> It's a massive lock.

>   **ROBERT**
> Too big for you to unlock, I mean
> you're so small.

Tom looks up at Robert, but says nothing. He starts to poke at the fire.

>   **MICHAEL**
> I can do it! I can unlock them.

>   **ROBERT**
> Can you? Well –

>   **LEIGH**
> This is all I could find.

Robert turns. Leigh has emerged from the woods.

>   **ROBERT**
> You know, it's rude to sneak up on a
> fellow like that, Leigh. I thought you
> was collecting wood. Why didn't
> you shout out, Tom?

>   **TOM**
> Didn't see him.

>   **ROBERT**
>   (menacing)
>   Really?
>
>   **LEIGH**
>   My mother will be wondering where
>   we are.

Robert stands. Leigh looks to Tom, who tenses. Robert looks between them. He grins.

>   **ROBERT**
>   You better get back then.

Leigh leads his younger brother away.

>   **ROBERT**
>   Be seeing you soon.

INT. LEIGH'S BEDROOM – NIGHT

Leigh lies in bed awake. At every creak from the house he flinches. He can hear something outside. Steps in the yard?

He slips from his bed.

INT. STAIRCASE – CONTINUOUS

Leigh pads down the stairs. Definitely steps outside.

INT. CUPBOARD – CONTINUOUS

Leigh opens a wooden chest and pulls out a cricket stump.

William Simpson

INT. BACK HALL – CONTINUOUS

Armed now, Leigh looks out the window.

The yard outside is illuminated by moonlight. A vague shape moving. There is someone out there.

Leigh crouches out of sight, gripping the stump.

INT. BACK HALL – DAWN

Leigh wakes with a start. He is huddled by the front door, cricket stump by his side. Upstairs he can hear his mother moving about. The house seems normal.

He rises and looks out the window. The yard is empty.

Leigh unlocks the front door, which immediately swings open as the weight of a body pushes it back.

Tom collapses backwards into the back hall.

      TOM
    Morning.

EXT. THE YARD – MORNING

Tom and Leigh sit on the wall outside, eating toast.

      TOM
    I had to make sure he wouldn't ... I
    didn't mean to scare you. He's gone
    his own way. He won't come back.

Leigh looks at him. There's clearly been a fight; Tom's fists are cut, his clothes torn. His feet are still bare.

>   **LEIGH**
>   I'll get you some shoes.

Leigh hops down and indicates for Tom to follow him.

>   **LEIGH**
>   Come on.

FADE OUT.

William Simpson was born in Dunstable, the Monaco of South Bedfordshire, and lives in Bedford, the Venice of North Bedfordshire. He studied Classics at the University of Cambridge where he wrote and acted in numerous plays, but never mastered the art of suitable geographical comparison.

Andrew Strike

Moving On

Blackness.

>   **CATHY (V.O.)**
>   This isn't what I wanted.

A single gun shot rings out.

>   **FADE IN:**

INT. KITCHEN – NIGHT

The floor is covered in shards of broken china and pasta shells. On a wall above a kitchen table is a large framed photo of RICHARD (28) and CATHY (25), they're sitting huddled together on steps that lead to a small beach. It's a bright sunny day and they're both smiling.

The glass of the photo frame is smeared with what could be blood and on the wall underneath is a huge blood-red splatter.

EXT. BEACH – MORNING – FLASH FORWARD

CATHY (52) and RICHARD (55) sit huddled together on a step. Richard pours steaming coffee from a thermos into a cup. He offers it to Cathy but she shakes her head. Richard sips the coffee slowly as he looks out to sea.

> **CATHY**
> You know I can't stay.

> **RICHARD**
> I know. I just wanted a proper goodbye.

Cathy digs into Richard's backpack and pulls out an urn which she hands to Richard.

> **CATHY**
> I do love it here.

> **RICHARD**
> Me too.

INT. SUSIE AND MARK'S LIVING ROOM – AFTERNOON – FLASHBACK

Richard and MARK (55) are standing in a large, immaculately decorated living room. Mark hands Richard an envelope.

> **MARK**
> We're all really sorry to see you go.

Richard doesn't respond; instead he turns the envelope round between his hands examining all sides.

> **MARK**
> Are you going to open it?

Richard seems in a daze, transfixed by the envelope.

> **RICHARD**
> Yes. Sorry.

Andrew Strike

Richard slowly opens the envelope and removes a small card. It reads: 'Enjoy your early retirement'. He opens the card and it's filled with little messages and well wishes.

RICHARD
Thanks. It means a lot.

Cathy enters carrying a tray of glasses followed by SUSIE (45) who is holding a bottle of champagne. Cathy hands out the glasses to Richard and Mark and Susie pours.

CATHY
Here's to retirement, new adventures and a lifetime of happiness. Cheers.

Everyone joins in with the toast.

Richard walks over to Cathy. He wraps his arms around her and kisses her cheek.

CATHY
Happy retirement, sweetheart.

Cathy and Richard share a tender embrace.

MARK
So what are you going to do now?

RICHARD
I don't know. Just take it easy. Relax a little. Maybe we'll do some travelling.
(looking into Cathy's eyes)
It will just be nice to spend some time together for once.

> **SUSIE**
> Well good luck to you both. You deserve it.

Susie downs the rest of her glass.

> **SUSIE**
> OK that's enough you two.

Susie separates Richard and Cathy.

> **SUSIE**
> Richard, you're with Mark. We're meeting you there; we have a slight detour to make.

> **RICHARD**
> Sounds suspicious.

Richard gives Cathy another quick kiss on the lips.

> **CATHY**
> Love you.

> **SUSIE**
> Go.

> **RICHARD**
> Love you, too.

Susie pushes Mark and Richard out the door and closes it behind her.

INT. RICHARD'S LIVING ROOM – DAY – FLASH FORWARD

A large living room inside a flat. In the middle of the room there are two large sofas that face each other, separated in the middle by a coffee table.

Richard struggles through the front door with two heavy carrier bags. He places the bags on the floor and begins to remove his coat, but stops as he notices a woman's coat already hanging on the hook. He lingers on it sadly; he strokes the arm of the jacket and closes his eyes.

INT. RICHARD'S LIVING ROOM – FLASHBACK

Richard, all smiles, walks in through the front door of the same apartment.

> **RICHARD**
> (calling)
> I'm home.

Richard takes off his coat and turns to hang it up.

> **CATHY (O.S.)**
> Just a minute.

As he turns back, he sees Cathy emerge from the kitchen. She's smiling as she rushes over, she wraps her arms round him and kisses him on the cheek. Richard embraces her tightly and strokes her arm as he squeezes his eyes shut.

EXT. HIGH STREET – AFTERNOON – FLASH FORWARD

Cathy emerges from a travel agent on a busy high street. She is looking round and eventually notices Susie's car parked across the street. She's excitedly waving an envelope in the air as she rushes over and isn't paying attention as she steps out into the road.

There's a screeching of tyres. Cathy turns to see the advancing car, a look of fear sweeps across her face.

INT. LIVING ROOM – FLASHBACK

Richard opens his eyes suddenly. He's hugging the woman's coat. He looks over towards the kitchen doorway and stares for a moment, waiting for someone to emerge. No one does.

EXT. PARK – MORNING – FLASH FORWARD

Richard walks alone through a quiet park.

There are a few YOUNG CHILDREN playing and an OLDER MAN walking a dog. On the path ahead Richard sees Susie approaching. She smiles and there's an awkward hug before they both sit down on a bench.

> **SUSIE**
> I'm glad you called.

> **RICHARD**
> I'm sorry. I just ... I didn't know what else to do.

> **SUSIE**
> How are you?

INT. KITCHEN – FLASHBACK PREVIOUS DAY

Richard stands in front of the oven, dishing out pasta into two separate bowls. He removes a pan from the hob and pours into the first bowl. As he comes to the second bowl, he freezes.

> **RICHARD (V.O.)**
> Everything I do reminds me ...

Richard suddenly snaps and hurls the pan across the room. It crashes against the wall spraying tomato sauce everywhere. He grabs the second bowl and smashes it against the floor. Pieces of china and pasta scatter everywhere.

Andrew Strike

> RICHARD (V.O.)
> She's not here.

EXT. PARK – MORNING – FLASH FORWARD

> SUSIE
> That's only natural. It will just take
> ... You just need to give yourself
> time.

> RICHARD
> I don't know what to do now. How
> do people get through this?

> SUSIE
> We just muddle through. Try to find
> something that gives us a little
> piece of happiness and hang onto it.

> RICHARD
> And if that doesn't work?

Susie considers for a moment and then takes Richard's hand in hers. She looks up and nods towards a passing dog.

> SUSIE
> We buy puppies.

Richard laughs. Susie gives him a hug.

INT. LIVING ROOM – NIGHT – PRESENT

Richard sits on the sofa, holding an envelope. After some hesitation he rips into the envelope. Inside he finds two tickets and a note.

INSERT:

Richard's POV: The note is unfolded. It says: 'Together we've seen the world, travelled the roads, and flown through the skies. Now let's get lost at sea.'

The tickets are for a 14-night Southern Caribbean Cruise, staying in a deluxe suite on a ship called 'Explorer Of The Seas'.

BACK TO SCENE

Richard folds the note and places it on the coffee table along with the tickets.

He stands and walks over to a cabinet in the corner of the room. He pulls open a drawer and searches through it, throwing various papers and photos on the floor. He finally finds what he's looking for – a small wooden box.

He walks back over to the sofa where he sits. He places the box on the coffee table and opens it. Inside the box is a gun.

Richard takes the gun from the box and stares at it.

>   CATHY (O.S.)
>   This isn't what I wanted.

Richard jumps, and the gun is fired.

INT. CREMATORIUM CHAPEL – DAY – FLASHBACK

At the front of a large airy chapel is a beautiful white coffin perched on a stand.

Rows of pews are filled with sad mourners. Richard sits alone on the front row. A MINISTER stands in front of the coffin reading from a Bible.

Richard is staring at the coffin in anguish, tears welling, his heart pounding. He can't watch anymore, he's heard enough. He stands and walks out, refusing to make eye contact with anyone. The congregation murmur amongst themselves.

EXT. CREMATORIUM – CONTINUOUS

Richard strides out of the building, hands pressed deeply into his pockets.

Mark is standing outside smoking. Richard stops as he sees him, and then continues. Mark follows him.

>   **MARK**
> Look Richard, I know you think this
> whole thing's just an empty ritual
> and you probably don't want to hear
> this, but it's important to remember
> that there's something out there.
> Something bigger than all this.
> Bigger than you and me.

Mark lunges forward and grabs Richard's arm.

>   **MARK**
> You will see her again. You'll be
> together again. You just have to
> have faith.

>   **RICHARD**
> You're right. I don't want to hear it.
> Now get your fucking hand off me.

Richard angrily pulls away from Mark's grasp.

>   **MARK**
> I was just trying to help.

Richard glares at Mark, then walks off towards his car.

INT. RICHARD'S CAR – CONTINUOUS

Susie appears at the driver's side window. Mark is behind her. She bangs on the window but Richard ignores her.

>   **SUSIE**
> Richard. Please. Come on! Don't
> leave like this. We love you. Let me
> help. Richard!

The window rolls down.

>   **RICHARD**
> Just leave me alone.

Richard drives off.

INT. LIVING ROOM – NIGHT – PRESENT

Cathy stands in the doorway. Richard is stunned.

>   **RICHARD**
> What the hell?

>   **CATHY**
> I came to check on you.

On the table Richard's mobile beeps. He can't take his eyes from Cathy.

>   **CATHY**
> Maybe you should get that?

Richard just stares, dumbfounded. Cathy walks over and picks up the phone and clicks on the text message.

Andrew Strike

                    CATHY
            It's Suze. You really should call her.
            She can help.

Richard, realising he still has the gun in his hand, places it back on the table. Cathy sits down and places the phone on the table next to the gun.

                    CATHY
            Do you believe in Heaven?

                    RICHARD
            What?

                    CATHY
            Heaven? White clouds, angels
            singing, harps playing?

                    RICHARD
            I don't want to have this
            conversation.

                    CATHY
            Well, what do you think's going to
            happen when you pull that trigger?

Richard shrugs.

                    CATHY (CONT'D)
            Do you think everything will just go
            black? Your body just rot in the
            ground?

Richard looks down and locks his hands behind the back of his neck.

                    CATHY (CONT'D)
            Or do you believe we'll be together

again? Reunited in some sort of paradise? Some new world we can explore together?

Richard's hands cover his ears as he tries to block out the questions.

CATHY (CONT'D)
I only ask because maybe it's an important consideration for someone who's planning to end his life.

Richard's hands ball into fists, his knuckles turning white.

RICHARD
(roaring)
You left me! You promised me a lifetime! And whatever's out there … Be it Heaven or Hell I don't care. Whatever it is has to be better than this!

Cathy looks at him, steadily. He won't look in her eyes.

CATHY
Why are you so scared?

RICHARD
(defensive)
I'm not scared of dying.

CATHY
Just of living.

Richard reaches out across the table to touch Cathy's hand.

EXT. BEACH – MORNING – FLASH FORWARD

The waves are lapping at Richard's ankles as he stands, head bowed. After a moment he glances over his shoulder and sees Cathy sitting on the steps watching him. He unscrews the cap from the urn. As he tips it the wind catches the ashes and sends them swirling into the air and out to sea. Richard smiles.

> **CATHY (O.S.)**
> I'll see you soon.

Richard glances over his shoulder again, but this time the steps are empty. Cathy is gone.

INT. RICHARD'S LIVING ROOM – NIGHT – PRESENT

Richard is alone. His hand is outstretched over the table and he sees that it is hovering over the gun. Tears welling, he reaches out. A tear runs down his face as he lifts his hand to his head.

> **SUSIE (O.S.)**
> Richard.

The gun is on the coffee table. In Richard's hand, pressed to his ear, he holds the mobile phone.

> **RICHARD**
> (into phone)
> Hi, Suze …

FADE OUT

Born in Huntingdon in 1982, **Andrew Strike** studied a BA in Media Studies and Journalism before moving to Norwich to study an MA in Scriptwriting. Married with four beautiful cats, he enjoys reading, loves foreign movies and is happiest when sat in a coffee shop with his wonderful wife Amber.

Moving On

Sunitha Webster

The Crowe Speaks
An Animated Short

INT. KITCHEN, THE CROWE HOUSE, LUDHAM BRIDGE – MORNING

LIBBY CROWE, 18, mixed-race, shuffles in. Hair scraped back, work-a-day clothes.

She grabs a biscuit, slides on her jacket. She goes to open the fridge but stops, seeing a new sticky-note on the door, among many creased ones. She peels it off.

INSERT

POV Libby: The sticky-note says:

Off for a couple of days. Cash in coffee jar if you need it. Mum.

BACK TO SCENE

Libby crumples and chucks the note. She inserts her MP3 earphones.

EXT. RIVER'S EDGE, LUDHAM BRIDGE – MORNING

NATHAN RAGGS, black, 24, lies on the grass. It is a warm, summer day. He reads a well-worn hardback.

INSERT

POV Nathan: A colour plate shows a stylised, lithe woman draped in a toga-like net, hair flowing over shoulders. Nathan's fingers slide down the page, not quite connecting with her contours.

BACK TO SCENE

Nathan sits up and closes the book gently.

EXT. WAYFARER'S CAFE, LUDHAM BRIDGE – MORNING

MUSIC – *Dance Wiv Me* by Dizzee Rascal plays on Libby's MP3 player. She wipes down outdoor table-tops. She dances and CUSTOMERS give the odd glance and smile. Several BIRDS perch nearby.

EXT. RIVER'S EDGE, LUDHAM BRIDGE – MORNING – CONTINUOUS

MUSIC – *Dance Wiv Me* by Dizzee Rascal can be heard faintly. Nathan – in waders – is peering over the water through binoculars.

EXT. RIVERSIDE, LUDHAM BRIDGE – MORNING – CONTINUOUS

MUSIC – *Dance Wiv Me* by Dizzee Rascal plays on a portable DAB radio. Beside it, CHRONIC RAGGS, black, 19, dances, sipping lager. He looks at Nathan and shakes his head.

EXT. WAYFARER'S CAFE, LUDHAM BRIDGE – MORNING – CONTINUOUS

Libby dances in sync with the flying birds. They land on her hand intermittently to pick up morsels and she launches them with a flourish when done. A few customers applaud.

MARTHA WAKEFIELD, late 40s, stands in the window of the café and beckons Libby in, glaring. She looks at the flying birds fitfully.

INT. WAYFARER'S CAFE, LUDHAM BRIDGE – MORNING – CONTINUOUS

Libby removes her headphones – the song emits in tinny tones.

> **MARTHA** (hissing)
> I've told you before about ... vermin.
> You're making a spectacle of yourself.
> I'm warning you, there's a limit.

Martha marches into the kitchen. Libby watches her.

EXT. RIVERSIDE, LUDHAM BRIDGE – MORNING – CONTINUOUS

The song sputters to a stop. Chronic picks up the DAB radio and shakes it. He sips from his bottle – it is empty. He chucks it.

Chronic approaches Nathan.

EXT. RIVER'S EDGE, LUDHAM BRIDGE – MORNING

Nathan views a KINGFISHER perching on a tree stump opposite. It turns and stares back.

He removes the binoculars. The kingfisher whizzes up and lands on a post a few feet away. It watches him.

Chronic taps Nathan on the shoulder.

> **CHRONIC**
> Let's go, bruv.

Nathan doesn't notice – he is too busy looking at the kingfisher.

> **CHRONIC (continued)**
> We're meant to be chillin'.

Nathan makes notes in a journal. Chronic sees Nathan watching the kingfisher.

> **CHRONIC (continued)**
> Can't believe you're passin' on me
> for that! It's like, a rat, with wings.

The kingfisher ascends and aims for Chronic, who freezes. At the last minute, Chronic tries to duck – but the splat finds its mark. Nathan creases up, laughing.

The kingfisher flies towards the Ludham Bridge shops.

EXT. WAYFARER'S CAFE, LUDHAM BRIDGE – MID-MORNING – CONTINUOUS

The kingfisher zooms onto a table that Libby is clearing, staring at her. She freezes momentarily, returning its stare. She recovers and heads down the alley, out of sight. The kingfisher follows.

EXT. NATHAN'S BOAT – EARLY AFTERNOON

Chronic is on deck, freshly showered, rubbing his hair with a towel. Nathan is sitting, reading the hardback from earlier.

> **NATHAN**
> You'll go bald.

> **CHRONIC**
> I'll sue you if I do, yeah? This is your
> fault. Filth on my head ... man, you
> owe me.

Chronic rubs harder with the towel. Nathan smiles and continues reading. Chronic grabs the hardback. Nathan sits back.

          CHRONIC
      Shops, pubs, people. Real girls even.
      Not flying rats. Or this book shit.
      Take a chance with some real stuff
      for once.

Nathan gets up, grabs back the book and picks up his binoculars. Chronic sighs. Nathan ignores him and sits.

          NATHAN
      Better get dressed then. If you want
      to see this real stuff.

EXT. BACK OF WAYFARER'S CAFE, LUDHAM BRIDGE – AFTERNOON

Libby stands in the shade of a large oak tree. The kingfisher is perched on a low branch. They are alone.

          LIBBY
      Charlie?

She stretches out her hand. The kingfisher, Charlie, flies to it. Libby strokes him. Charlie preens.

          CHARLIE
      An announcement. I have found
      your mate.

          LIBBY
      Yeah right!

She sends him flying and turns to go back. Charlie lands on the ground in front of her.

> **CHARLIE**
> Wait, I'll show you what I've seen, my dear!

She tries to proceed but he mobs her.

> **LIBBY**
> All right, Jesus!

> **CHARLIE**
> Right hand on my head, close your eyes. You know the routine.

Libby shrugs.

> **CHARLIE (continued)**
> A little enthusiasm, my dear.

With some reluctance, Libby complies. She rests her hand on his head.

EXT. RIVER ANT – MORNING – FLASHBACK – CONTINUOUS

Libby's eyes fly open.

INSERT

POV Libby: She hovers above the river. At the shore, she sees Nathan viewing her through binoculars. She flies to him. She watches him.

END OF FLASHBACK

BACK TO SCENE

Libby comes to.

EXT. BACK OF WAYFARER'S CAFE, LUDHAM BRIDGE – AFTERNOON – CONTINUOUS

She sees Charlie darting about.

> **CHARLIE**
> So my dear. Verdict?

Libby paces and kicks up dust. Charlie lands on a low branch. She sits.

> **CHARLIE**
> You saw him ...

> **LIBBY**
> No, you saw him. I didn't.

Charlie cheeps. He lands on her lap.

> **CHARLIE**
> I know you like him, Libby.
> Remember, nothing ventured –

The sound of a bucket of water splashing into a gutter interrupts them. Seconds later, a loud scream sends Charlie flying off.

> **MARTHA**
> That's it, I can't take it any more!
> That, creature ... again! You're fired!

Martha darts inside before Libby can speak.

EXT. RIVERSIDE FOOTPATH, LUDHAM BRIDGE – AFTERNOON

Libby sits on the grass, staring at the river. On the ground lie several crumpled-up pieces of paper. She puts a notebook in her pocket. She buries her head in her arms.

Nathan and Chronic emerge from around the corner. Chronic nudges Nathan and nods in her direction. Nathan tries to go back but Chronic steers him forward. They arrive and Nathan stands with arms crossed.

>   **CHRONIC**
>   Hi.

Libby scoots back a little, startled.

>   **CHRONIC**
>   I'm Chronic.

She rises and pulls her jacket tight. She and Nathan look at each other for a long moment – Chronic notices.

>   **LIBBY**
>   I've got to be going.

>   **CHRONIC**
>   Wait, wait ... talk to my brother and that. He's like ... into countryside and shit.

She walks away.

>   **CHRONIC (shouting)**
>   We'll be at The Dog Inn!

When she's out of sight Nathan claps, slowly.

>   **NATHAN**
>   Mr Ladykiller.

>   **CHRONIC**
>   Mr Shutyourmouth. Least I had the guts to open mine.

Chronic picks up a piece of paper and unfolds it.

INSERT

POV Chronic: An expert pencil sketch of a kingfisher.

BACK TO SCENE

Chronic chucks it.

>CHRONIC
>Shit

Chronic walks on. Nathan retrieves the picture and regards it.

INT. LIBBY'S BEDROOM – EARLY EVENING

Cramped but tidy. Libby sits on the bed in glam, sleeveless top and low-rider jeans. Her hair is all volume, face glowing. She hugs her shawl to her face – it's iridescent, mesh-like.

Charlie lands on the windowsill. She lets him in.

>CHARLIE
>I'm sorry, my dear. About your job.

She shrugs it off. He hops onto her hand and she lifts him. They are face-to-face.

>CHARLIE (continued)
>He's still out there. Why are you waiting?

>LIBBY
>I just …

>CHARLIE
>You don't have to be afraid.

Sunitha Webster

Charlie flies back to the windowsill.

> **CHARLIE**
> Just have the courage to try.
> Goodbye Libby, my dear.

> **LIBBY**
> Charlie?

> **CHARLIE**
> It's time for you to fly alone.

She scrambles towards him but he flies away. She sits on the edge of the bed, hugging herself. She straightens up and takes a deep breath. She wraps herself in her shawl, grabs her bag and leaves.

EXT. WAYFARER'S CAFE, LUDHAM BRIDGE – EVENING

Libby hurries past the café but stops when she hears Martha's screams. Martha tries to lock up but a flock of birds mobs her when she does. Libby smiles, shakes her head and whistles. The birds whistle back and leave. Martha cowers on the ground.

EXT. THE DOG INN, LUDHAM BRIDGE – EVENING

Libby sees Nathan alone at an outdoor table with two pint glasses – his half-full, the other empty. She strokes her shawl a moment and approaches him.

> **LIBBY**
> Hi.

Nathan knocks his glass and his hands get wet; he shakes them off. Droplets of beer fly into Libby's face as she sits. She finds a tissue to clean up.

                    NATHAN
         Oh, shit, sorry.

                    LIBBY
         That's all right.

Nathan looks round desperately, grabs beer-mats and tries to mop up the spill. Libby puts her hand on his arm.

                    LIBBY
         It's OK. Honest.

She gets more tissues and clears up. Nathan relaxes and sips from his glass.

                    LIBBY
         I'm Libby, by the way.

She holds out her hand. He holds on a moment longer than necessary.

                    NATHAN
         Nathan.

He realises something and pulls the papers he collected out of his pocket.

                    NATHAN
         You left these.

She clasps the edge of the table.

                    NATHAN (continued)
         I was wondering if I could ... keep
         them ... it's just ... you left them
         and that. They're amazing.

Libby smiles and nods. Chronic appears in the pub doorway with two

Sunitha Webster

more pints. He sees the two of them and reverses.

> **NATHAN**
> Just got a question, request, really.
> The bittern you drew. You seen one?
> Real-life?

> **LIBBY**
> Yeah.

Libby fiddles with her shawl.

> **LIBBY (continued)**
> I can take you there. If you want.

Nathan nods. Libby goes. He sees his hardback book and binoculars on the table. He hesitates.

> **CHRONIC (V.O.)**
> Take a chance with some real stuff
> for once.

Nathan runs to join Libby. Book and binoculars remain.

EXT. ST. BENET'S ABBEY – NIGHT

Rough, tussocky grassland broken in the distance by the odd hedge or lone tree. A sky full of stars.

The decayed stone arch of the abbey gatehouse encloses a dominant, red-brick windmill. To the south is the river Bure, reeds swaying. Nothing else except the stubs of the old abbey precinct.

EXT. WESTERN RIVERSIDE, ST. BENET'S ABBEY – NIGHT

Libby and Nathan stand at the water's edge, his boat moored beside them. Libby points to a small tree amidst the reeds. Nathan is too busy taking in the abbey to notice.

> **NATHAN**
> This place ... it's something else.

> **LIBBY**
> Yeah.

She takes his hand and they walk towards the main arch.

EXT. ARCH, ST. BENET'S ABBEY – NIGHT

Nathan runs his hands over the arch – dressed sandstone blocks.

Libby smiles at him and goes into the windmill.

The blocks are engraved with a mess of names and dates. Some are distinct. Nathan reads.

INSERT

Nathan's POV: The text says:

Ray & Jane 2004.

BACK TO SCENE

Nathan runs his fingers over the names.

INT. WINDMILL, ST. BENET'S ABBEY – NIGHT

Libby steps forward, looks up at the moon and slips, hitting her shoulder against the brick wall.

                    LIBBY
            Shit!

EXT. ARCH, ST. BENET'S ABBEY – NIGHT – CONTINUOUS

Her cry startles Nathan who stumbles into a run through the arch, into the inner doorway of the windmill.

INT. WINDMILL, ST. BENET'S ABBEY – NIGHT – CONTINUOUS

Nathan sees her and stops.

She is framed by the inner arch, moonlit. The mesh shawl is draped over one shoulder. The other is grazed.

She holds her head up, looks away. She is shivering.

                    LIBBY
            Stupid … I'm sorry.

He approaches slowly. He runs his fingers over the grazes. He kisses her shoulder. He unzips his jacket and puts it over her.

She slides her arm out from his grasp. He looks at her, searching. She places her hands on his face and pulls him to her. They kiss.

In the distance, the boom-boom call of a bird sounds and fades.

THE END

Sunitha Webster studied biology initially and worked in various roles, including Extras Co-ordinator on a feature film. She studied animation production at London College of Printing and first studied creative writing at Birkbeck College, specialising in theatre. She was fortunate in being selected as the Skillset Screenwriting Bursary holder for 2008/2009.